The Book of Quotes

The Book of QUOTES

Barbara Rowes

A Sunrise Book

E. P. DUTTON·NEW YORK

ACKNOWLEDGMENTS

For helping with research and additional source materials: Adam Fensterheim, Jeanette Freeman, Susie Greenberg, John Sauer, Susan Sontag, Heidi Howell, Jackie Kaukonen, Judy Thompson, Dennis Miller, Stu Ginsburg, Herb Hellman, Carol Ross, Celeste Huston, and Russ Woodgates.

With special acknowledgment to the New York Public Library for their research facilities; to *Forbes, Vogue,* and NBC for permission to do research in their libraries; to Brian Cox for assistance with technical problems; to Judy Kazsyl for a calming influence; to Carol Guardino for support. For permission to use photographs: NASA, RCA Corporation, Atlantic Records, *People* magazine, David Gahr. For permission to review transcripts: Edith Luray, the "Beverly Sills Show"; Marjorie Germane and Madeline Amgott, "Not For Women Only." And to Harry, for believing every speaker needs a book of quotes.

For information contact: E. P. Dutton, 2 Park Avenue, New York, N.Y. 10016

Library of Congress Cataloging in Publication Data
Main entry under title: The Book of Quotes. Includes index.
1. United States—Social conditions—1960— —Quotations, maxims, etc.
I. Rowes, Barbara. HN65.A682 1979 309.1'73'092 78-10891 ISBN: 0-87690-343-X

Published simultaneously in Canada by Clarke, Irwin & Company Limited, Toronto and Vancouver

Designed by Barbara Huntley   10 9 8 7 6 5 4 3 2 1   First Edition

*To Marge and John
for their friendship*

With special appreciation to Marilyn E. Mason
for her undying labor,
Campbell Geeslin for his encouragement,
Father Walter Ong for his guidance,
Marshall McLuhan for his wit,
Martin Bernheimer for his instruction,
Joanna Krotz for her faith,
Jeremy Nussbaum for his counsel
and
Nancy Crawford, my editor,
for her high standards and commitment.

Contents

A Note about Quotes

—**Aristotle Onassis, J. Paul Getty,** and **Ralph Nader** on business

—**Yves Saint Laurent** and **Diana Vreeland** on style

—**Henry Kissinger** and **Bella Abzug** on politics

—**Elizabeth Ray** on sexual politics

—**Julia Child** and **Euell Gibbons** on food

—**Archibald Cox** and **Martha Mitchell** on Watergate

—**Neil Armstrong** on space

—**General William Westmoreland** and **Dr. Spock** on Vietnam

—**Burt Reynolds** on *machismo*

—**Beverly Sills** and **George Balanchine** on the arts

—**Anaïs Nin** and **Truman Capote** on literature

—**The Beatles** and **Allen Ginsberg** on rock

—**Dr. Martin Luther King, Jr.,** and **Abbie Hoffman** on liberation

—**Mario Savio, Erik Erikson,** and **Gail Sheehy** on the generation gap

—**Marabel Morgan** on femininity

—**Gloria Steinem** and **Phyllis Schlafly** on women's rights

—**Woody Allen** and **Lily Tomlin** on humor

—**JFK, LBJ, Richard Nixon, Gerald Ford,** and **Jimmy Carter** on the Presidency

—**Barbra Streisand** and **Ken Kesey** on Hollywood

—**Spiro T. Agnew** and **Marshall McLuhan** on the media

—**Billy Graham** and **Werner Erhard** on spirituality

—**Muhammad Ali** on Muhammad Ali . . .

and much more

IN THESE PAGES, the reflections of contemporary American society are translated into a modern shorthand of ideas; a profound, moving, and often hilarious collection of varied sensibilities, expressions, trends, and pop ideologies from the mouths of those who have done the most to shape our culture. In short, a people's book of quotes from the most influential figures of our time.

From John Bartlett's nineteenth-century roundup to recent collections of quotations, the quote has traditionally been relegated to a small corner of our literary appreciation—in volumes of high-level anthologies destined to collect dust on the shelf. Readers of quote books have always turned to these volumes of classical wit and ideology for little more than moments of idle amusement, or, at best, reference. Seldom, if ever, has a book of quotations reflected its own time or been read cover-to-cover, much as one would read an absorbing novel.

Today, however, as a result of the general cultural awakening of the last twenty years and the pervading influence of multimedia in our society, we no longer need to wait for the future to understand the impact of the present. Instead, we readily turn to the words of our contemporary philosophers, such as Marshall McLuhan, Susan Sontag, and Buckminster Fuller, for our understanding of ourselves and our experiences in the world around us. Their instamatic expressions have drawn the quotation out of its corner and into the foreground of print.

The Book of Quotes is the first comprehensive recapping of the major events, ideas, and personalities of our time—a verbal history of current events that re-creates the contemporary scenes, trends, and epiphanic moments that have contributed to the growth and new directions of our American culture.

New York City, November, 1978   Barbara Rowes

The Book of Quotes

1
—————————————————————
Kennedy

ON JANUARY 20, 1961, forty-three-year-old John Fitzgerald Kennedy was sworn in as the thirty-fifth president of the United States. As the first Catholic president, he embodied the spirit of democratic equality, and as the youngest man ever elected to the nation's highest office, he revitalized an apathetic people and inspired high principles with his vision of the New Frontier.

Along with his elegant wife Jacqueline, Kennedy breathed new life into the ancient myth of Camelot, ushering in an unprecedented era of culture and sophistication in the White House. Robert Frost was uncrowned poet laureate of the country; Pablo Casals came to play. Physical fitness grew into a national issue—with the handsome young president playing a tough offense at the family touch-football games in Hyannisport. A spirit of growing optimism reigned.

Kennedy's foreign policy became the brunt of sharp criticism after his ill-fated invasion of the Bay of Pigs, but his verve and cultivated good wit seemed to keep his greatest admirers—the American people—close by his side. Still, darkness was in store. On November 22, 1963, the American dream plummeted into a national nightmare. While riding through the streets of Dallas in an open limousine, Kennedy was shot to death by two sniper bullets. Lee Harvey Oswald was arrested for the assassination, then murdered by Jack Ruby in a Dallas police station as a traumatized America watched on television.

We stand today on the edge of a new frontier.
—**John F. Kennedy,** July 15, 1960

The new frontier of which I speak is not a set of promises—it is a set of challenges. It sums up not what I intend to offer to the American people, but what I intend to ask of them. . . . It appeals to our pride, not our security—it holds out the promise of more sacrifice instead of more security.
—**John F. Kennedy**

Ask not what your country can do for you; ask what you can do for your country.
—**John F. Kennedy**

All this will not be finished in the first one hundred days. Nor will it be finished in the first one thousand days, not in the life of this administration, nor even perhaps in our lifetime on this planet.
—**John F. Kennedy**

Let us never negotiate out of fear, but let us never fear to negotiate.
—**John F. Kennedy,** Inaugural address, January 20, 1961

History is a relentless master. It has no present, only the past rushing into the future. To try to hold fast is to be swept aside.
—**John F. Kennedy**

The United States has to move very fast to even stand still.
—**John F. Kennedy**

There will always be dissident voices heard in the land, expressing opposition without alternatives, finding fault but never favor, perceiving gloom on every side and seeking influence without responsibility. Those voices are inevitable. But today other voices are heard in the land—voices preaching doctrines wholly unrelated to reality, wholly unsuited to the sixties, doctrines which apparently assume that words will suffice without weapons, that vituperation is as good as victory, and that peace is a sign of weakness.
—**John F. Kennedy**

One fifth of the people are against everything all the time.
—Robert F. Kennedy

Those who make peaceful revolution impossible will make violent revolution inevitable.
—John F. Kennedy

There may be thousands of Americans more qualified to be president than me, but the choice is between two: Nixon and myself.
—John F. Kennedy

This week I had the opportunity to debate with Mr. Nixon. I feel that I should reveal that I had a great advantage in that debate. . . . Mr. Nixon had just debated with Khrushchev, and I had debated with Hubert Humphrey, and that gave me the edge.
—John F. Kennedy

I have the best of both worlds. A Harvard education and a Yale degree.
—John F. Kennedy, after receiving an honorary Yale degree

My son was rocked to political lullabies.
—Rose Kennedy

If you bungle raising your children, I don't think whatever else you do well matters very much.
—Jacqueline Kennedy

Mothers all want their sons to grow up to be president, but they don't want them to become politicians in the process!
—John F. Kennedy

A lot of women have been the mother of one president, but there never has been the mother of two or three presidents.
—Rose Kennedy

I had announced earlier this year that if successful I would not consider campaign contributions as a substitute for experience in appointing ambassadors. Ever since I made that statement, I have not received one single cent from my father.
—John F. Kennedy

I have just received the following telegram from my generous Daddy. It says, "Dear Jack: Don't buy a single vote more than is necessary. I'll be damned if I'm going to pay for a landslide."
—John F. Kennedy

We don't want any losers around. In this family we want winners.
—Joseph P. Kennedy

Let the word go forth from this time and place, to friend and foe alike, that the torch has been passed to a new generation of Americans—born in this century, tempered by war, disciplined by a hard and bitter peace.
—John F. Kennedy

I am one person who can truthfully say, "I got my job through the *New York Times.*"
—John F. Kennedy

When we got into office, the thing that surprised me most was to find that things were just as bad as we'd been saying they were.
—John F. Kennedy

It has recently been observed that whether I serve one or two terms in the presidency, I will find myself at the end of that period at what might be called the awkward age—too old to begin a career and too young to write my memoirs.
—John F. Kennedy

I understand Jacqueline Kennedy has redone the White House in eighteenth-century style. Why, then, I'd fit in perfectly.
—Barry Goldwater

Washington is a city of southern efficiency and northern charm.
—John F. Kennedy

I do not think it entirely inappropriate to introduce myself to this audience. I am the man who accompanied Jacqueline Kennedy to Paris, and I have enjoyed it.
—John F. Kennedy

What does my hair-do have to do with my husband's ability to be president?
—Jacqueline Kennedy

If there were anything I could take back to France with me, it would be Mrs. Kennedy.
—**Charles de Gaulle**

I couldn't spend that much unless I wore sable underwear.
—**Jacqueline Kennedy,** after being accused of spending $30,000 a year on her wardrobe

Is there such a thing as Shoppers Anonymous?
—**John F. Kennedy,** on receiving a $40,000 bill for his wife's clothes

I've had an exciting life. I married for love and got a little money along with it.
—**Rose Kennedy**

If we cannot now end our differences, at least we can help make the world safe for diversity.
—**John F. Kennedy**

I believe in an America where separation of church and state is absolute—where no Catholic prelate would tell the president (should he be a Catholic) how to act and no Protestant minister would tell his parishioners for whom to vote.
—**John F. Kennedy**

If a free society cannot help the many who are poor, it cannot save the few who are rich.
—**John F. Kennedy**

Mankind must put an end to war, or war will put an end to mankind.
—**John F. Kennedy,** United Nations address, September 25, 1961

Victory has a hundred fathers, and defeat is an orphan.
—**John F. Kennedy**

My brother Bob doesn't want to be in government—he promised Dad he'd go straight.
—**John F. Kennedy**

It isn't that I'm a saint. It's just that I've never found it necessary to be a sinner.
—**Robert F. Kennedy**

I don't see what's wrong with giving Bobby a little experience before he starts to practice law.
—**John F. Kennedy,** after appointing his brother Attorney General

Whenever men take the law into their own hands, the loser is the law. And when the law loses, freedom languishes.
—**Robert F. Kennedy**

I should like to love my country and still love justice.
—**Robert F. Kennedy,** quoting Albert Camus

Some men see things as they are and ask, "Why?" I dream things that never were and ask, "Why not?"
—**Robert F. Kennedy,** paraphrasing George Bernard Shaw

My views on birth control are somewhat distorted by the fact that I was seventh of nine children.
—**Robert F. Kennedy**

You have to have been a Republican to know how good it is to be a Democrat.
—**Jacqueline Kennedy**

I think this is the most extraordinary collection of talent, of human knowledge, that has ever been gathered together at the White House—with the possible exception of when Thomas Jefferson dined alone.
—**John F. Kennedy,** at a dinner for Nobel Prize winners, April 29, 1962

Jackie is like a little bird that needs its freedom as well as its security, and she gets them both from me.
—**Aristotle Onassis**

I can see her in about ten years from now on the yacht of a Greek petrol millionaire.
—**Charles de Gaulle,** on Jacqueline Kennedy

First I lost my weight, then I lost my voice, and now I lost Onassis.
—**Maria Callas**

Why did he marry that Jackie? She is ugly, with horrible legs, the skin of a hen, fat in the wrong places, and eyes too far apart from one another. She's a big nothing.
—**Litsa Calogeropoulos,** Maria Callas' mother

The American public would forgive me anything except running off with Eddie Fisher.
—**Jacqueline Kennedy**

We would like to live as we once lived, but history will not permit it.
—**John F. Kennedy**

Who knows whether any of us will still be alive in 1972? Existence is so fickle, fate is so fickle.
—**Robert F. Kennedy,** 1967

Just as I went into politics because Joe died, if anything happened to me tomorrow, Bobby would run for my seat in the Senate. And if Bobby died, our younger brother Teddy would take over for him.
—**John F. Kennedy**

I'm only interested in getting re-elected to the Senate.
—**Edward M. Kennedy,** September 1, 1975

I've been very close to the presidency. I don't see it as glamorous. . . . It's tough. It's risk-taking. It's everything I find unattractive.
—**Joan Kennedy**

If anyone is crazy enough to want to kill a president of the United States, he can do it. All he must be prepared to do is give his life for the president's.
—**John F. Kennedy**

I'm forty-three years old, and I'm the healthiest candidate for president in the United States. You've traveled with me enough to know that. I'm not going to die in office.
—**John F. Kennedy**

If somebody wants to shoot me from a window with a rifle, nobody can stop it, so why worry about it?
—**John F. Kennedy,** to his wife, November 22, 1963, in his Fort Worth hotel room before the assassination

I shouted out, "Who killed the Kennedys?" when after all, it was you and me.
—**Mick Jagger**

He was a lonely person. He trusted no one. He was too sick. It was the fantasy of a sick person, to get attention only for himself.
—**Marina Oswald,** on Lee Harvey Oswald

We develop the kind of citizens we deserve.
—**Robert F. Kennedy**

Truth is the only client here.
—**Unofficial motto** of the Warren Commission

The only thing we learn from history is that we do not learn.
—**Earl Warren**

> Now he is a legend when he would have preferred to be a man.
> —**Jacqueline Kennedy**
>
>
>
> UNITED PRESS INTERNATIONAL PHOTO

2
"Establishment"

IN A 1955 ARTICLE for the *Spectator*, British journalist Henry Fairlie coined the phrase "the Establishment." Ten years later, American hippies revived the term to describe their number one enemy—the power brokers of corporate society. In 1978, of the world's six largest corporations, five (Exxon—annual sales $48.6 billion, General Motors—$47.2 billion, Ford—$28.8 billion, Texaco—$26.5 billion, and Mobil—$26.1 billion) were American, proving that nothing surpasses American ingenuity in the pursuit of the sacred dollar.

There's no such thing as a free lunch.
—Milton Friedman

In a hierarchy every employee tends to rise to his level of incompetence.
—Laurence Peter

Nothing is illegal if one hundred businessmen decide to do it.
—Andrew Young

I don't meet competition. I crush it.
—**Charles Revson**

It's not enough that I should succeed—others should fail.
—**David Merrick**

It is ridiculous to call this an industry. This is not. This is rat eat rat, dog eat dog. I'll kill 'em, and I'm going to kill 'em before they kill me. You're talking about the American way of survival of the fittest.
—**Ray Kroc,** chairman of McDonald's

The individual choice of garnishment of a burger can be an important point to the consumer in this day when individualism, in my mind, is an increasingly important thing to people.
—**Donald N. Smith,** president of Burger King

I could eat hamburgers three times a day. It gets so your blood turns to ketchup.
—**Jerry Pelletier,** assistant dean of Hamburger University

Sacred cows make great hamburgers.
—**Robert Reisner**

There's no reason to be the richest man in the cemetery. You can't do any business from there.
—**Colonel Sanders**

If you can count your money, you don't have a billion dollars.
—**J. Paul Getty**

Finance is the art of passing currency from hand to hand until it finally disappears.
—**Robert W. Sarnoff**

A study of economics usually reveals that the best time to buy anything is last year.
—**Marty Allen**

So you think that money is the root of all evil. Have you ever asked what is the root of money?
—**Ayn Rand**

In this country, when you attack the Establishment, they don't put you in jail or a mental institution. They do something worse. They make you a member of the Establishment.
—**Art Buchwald**

You may give us your symptoms. We will make the diagnosis. And we, the Establishment—for which I make no apologies for being a part of—will implement the crime.
—**Spiro T. Agnew**

Hell hath no fury like a bureaucrat scorned.
—**Milton Friedman**

All currency is neurotic currency.
—**Norman O. Brown**

The entire essence of America is the hope to first make money— then make money with money—then make lots of money with lots of money.
—**Paul Erdman**

The more money an American accumulates, the less interesting he becomes.
—**Gore Vidal**

The man who tips a shilling every time he stops for petrol is giving away annually the cost of lubricating his car.
—**J. Paul Getty**

Don't complain. Don't explain.
—**Henry Ford II**

Never get angry. Never make a threat. Reason with people.
—**Don Corleone,** in *The Godfather*

The rich are different from you and me because they have more credit.
—**John Leonard**

An ounce of hypocrisy is worth a pound of ambition.
—**Michael Korda**

The cost of living is going up and the chance of living is going down.
—**Flip Wilson**

Inflation is the one form of taxation that can be imposed without legislation.
—**Milton Friedman**

Inflation is bringing us true democracy. For the first time in history, luxuries and necessities are selling at the same price.
—**Robert Orben,** professional gag writer for United States
    presidents

Insurance is death on the installment plan.
—**Philip Slater**

The reason why worry kills more people than work is that more people worry than work.
—**Robert Frost**

UNITED PRESS INTERNATIONAL PHOTO

Can you buy friendship? You not only can, you must. It's the *only* way to obtain friends. . . . Everything worthwhile has a price.
—**Robert J. Ringer**

A team is a mutual protection society formed to guarantee that no one person can be to blame for a botched committee job that one man could have performed satisfactorily.
—**Russell Baker**

The dynamics of capitalism is postponement of enjoyment to the constantly postponed future.
—**Norman O. Brown**

There are really not many jobs that actually require a penis or a vagina, and all other occupations should be open to everyone.
—**Gloria Steinem**

Young wives are the leading asset of corporate power. They want the suburbs, a house, a settled life. And respectability. They want society to see that they have exchanged themselves for something of value.
—**Ralph Nader**

To be successful, a woman has to be much better at her job than a man.
—**Golda Meir**

We're not going after their jobs, as long as they do their jobs and do not want to come out of the closet.
—**Anita Bryant**

We are confronted with insurmountable opportunities.
—**Pogo**

Nothing recedes like success.
—**Walter Winchell**

Try not to become a man of success but rather try to become a man of value.
—**Albert Einstein**

If it keeps up, man will atrophy all his limbs but the push-button finger.
—**Frank Lloyd Wright**

I bomb, therefore I am.
—**Philip Slater**

Technology or perish.
—**John R. Pierce,** executive director of Bell Laboratories

If technology is a church . . . then Ralph Nader is its first saint.
—**Charles McCarry**

I am responsible for my actions, but who is responsible for those of General Motors?
—**Ralph Nader**

Technological progress has merely provided us with more efficient means for going backwards.
—**Aldous Huxley**

Our Age of Anxiety is, in great part, the result of trying to do today's job with yesterday's tools.
—**Marshall McLuhan**

The robot is going to lose. Not by much. But when the final score is tallied, flesh and blood is going to beat the damn monster.
—**Adam Smith**

All power is vested in the people, public servants are your trustees. . . . We're turkeys for the utilities, and I'm tired of being plucked.
—**Henry Howell**

The Con Ed system is in the best shape in fifteen years, and there's no problem about the summer.
—**Charles Frank Luce,** chairman of Consolidated Edison, hours before the New York City blackout, July 1977

The computer is a moron.
—**Peter Drucker**

I do not fear computers. I fear the lack of them.
—**Isaac Asimov**

There are no new forms of financial fraud; in the last several hundred years, there have only been small variations on a few classic designs.
—**John Kenneth Galbraith**

Look, we trade every day out there with hustlers, deal-makers, shysters, con men. . . . That's the way businesses get started. That's the way this country was built.
—**Herbert Allen,** financier

The incestuous relationship between government and big business thrives in the dark.
—**Jack Anderson**

Wealth is the product of man's capacity to think.
—**Ayn Rand**

It takes brains not to make money. Any fool can make money. . . . But what about people with talent and brains?
—**Joseph Heller,** in *Catch-22*

Choice has always been a privilege of those who could afford to pay for it.
—**Ellen Frankfort**

The buck stops with the guy who signs the checks.
—**Rupert Murdoch**

Money is the barometer of a society's virtue.
—**Ayn Rand**

The fastest way to succeed is to look as if you're playing by other people's rules, while quietly playing by your own.
—**Michael Korda**

If you make a living, if you earn your own money, you're free—however free one can be on this planet.
—**Theodore White**

One cannot walk through a mass-production factory and not feel that one is in Hell.
—**W. H. Auden**

Absence of Quality is the essence of squareness.
—**Robert Pirsig**

I don't know the key to success, but the key to failure is trying to please everybody.
—**Bill Cosby**

Sometimes I worry about being a success in a mediocre world.
—**Lily Tomlin**

Gross National Product is our Holy Grail.
—**Stewart Udall**

The taxpayer—that's someone who works for the federal government but doesn't have to take a civil service examination.
—**Ronald Reagan**

Tax reform means, "Don't tax you, don't tax me. Tax that fellow behind the tree."
—**Russell Long**

The hardest thing in the world to understand is the income tax.
—**Albert Einstein**

If my business was legitimate, I would deduct a substantial percentage for depreciation of my body.
—**Xaviera Hollander**

Today, it takes more brains and effort to make out the income-tax form than it does to make the income.
—**Alfred E. Neuman**

Bing doesn't pay an income tax any more. He just asks the government what they need.
—**Bob Hope**

Work is a necessity for man. Man invented the alarm clock.
—**Pablo Picasso**

Going to work for a large company is like getting on a train. Are you going sixty miles an hour or is the train going sixty miles an hour and you're just sitting still?
—**J. Paul Getty**

A vacation is what you take when you can no longer take what you've been taking.
—**Earl Wilson**

When you have 7 percent unemployed, you have 93 percent working.
—**John F. Kennedy**

The brain is a wonderful organ; it starts working the moment you get up in the morning and does not stop until you get into the office.
—**Robert Frost**

Few great men could pass Personnel.
—**Paul Goodman**

Opportunities are usually disguised as hard work, so most people don't recognize them.
—**Ann Landers**

Some men are born mediocre, some men achieve mediocrity, and some men have mediocrity thrust upon them.
—**Joseph Heller**

I've always been worried about people who are willing to work for nothing. Sometimes that's all you get from them, nothing.
—**Sam Ervin**

I'm self-employed.
—**Prince Philip**

It's so American to start one's own business.
—**Anne McDonnell Ford**

There are an enormous number of managers who have retired on the job.
—**Peter Drucker**

Sooner or later I'm going to die, but I'm not going to retire.
—**Margaret Mead**

Retirement at sixty-five is ridiculous. When I was sixty-five I still had pimples.
—George Burns

Yesterday I was a dog. Today I'm a dog. Tomorrow I'll probably still be a dog. Sigh. There's so little hope for advancement.
—Snoopy

I'm not a member of any establishment. I'm too intuitional for the intellectuals and too conservative for the way out.
—Edward Albee

If you think nobody cares if you're alive, try missing a couple of car payments.
—Earl Wilson

The trouble with being poor is that it takes up all your time.
—Willem de Kooning

I'd like to live like a poor man with lots of money.
—Pablo Picasso

Poverty is expensive to maintain.
—Michael Harrington

By working faithfully eight hours a day, you may eventually get to be a boss and work twelve hours a day.
—Robert Frost

Civilization is unbearable, but it is *less* unbearable at the top.
—Timothy Leary

It is tragic that Howard Hughes had to die to prove that he was alive.
—Walter Kane

An honest man is one who knows that he can't consume more than he has produced.
—Ayn Rand

I have no money, no resources, no hopes. I am the happiest man alive.
—**Henry Miller**

We can never have enough of that which we really do not want.
—**Eric Hoffer**

Money is like manure. You have to spread it around or it smells.
—**J. Paul Getty**

The world at large does not judge us by who we are and what we know; it judges us by what we have.
—**Dr. Joyce Brothers**

Credit buying is much like being drunk. The buzz happens immediately, and it gives you a lift. . . . The hangover comes the day after.
—**Dr. Joyce Brothers**

In its famous paradox, the equation of money and excrement, psychoanalysis becomes the first science to state what common sense and the poets have long known—that the essence of money is in its absolute worthlessness.
—**Norman O. Brown**

There is a certain Buddhistic calm that comes from having . . . money in the bank.
—**Tom Robbins**

The man who damns money has obtained it dishonorably; the man who respects it has earned it.
—**Ayn Rand**

People who bite the hand that feeds them usually lick the boot that kicks them.
—**Eric Hoffer**

The best minds are not in government. If any were, business would hire them away.
—**Ronald Reagan**

The government solution to a problem is usually as bad as the problem.
—**Milton Friedman**

The genius of our ruling class is that it has kept a majority of the people from ever questioning the inequity of a system where most people drudge along, paying heavy taxes for which they get nothing in return.
—**Gore Vidal**

People of privilege will always risk their complete destruction rather than surrender any material part of their advantage.
—**John Kenneth Galbraith**

I have observed there is a difference between the Irish Mafia and the Texas Mafia. You may still receive the knife but you get prayed over in the process.
—**Eric Sevareid**

When have I ever refused an accommodation?
—**Don Corleone,** in *The Godfather*

To succeed it is necessary to accept the world as it is and rise above it.
—**Michael Korda**

Americans are broad-minded people. They'll accept the fact that a person can be an alcoholic, a dope fiend, a wife beater, and even a newspaperman, but if a man doesn't drive, there is something wrong with him.
—**Art Buchwald**

The secret and the difference between winners and losers is in discipline. The winner manages his money. The loser lets the money manage him.
—**Nicholas ("Nick The Greek") Dandalos**

A bank is a place where they lend you an umbrella in fair weather and ask for it back again when it begins to rain.
—**Robert Frost**

Foundations of a new religion can be laid only with the blessing of bankers.
—**Salvador Dali**

Banking may well be a career from which no man really recovers.
—**John Kenneth Galbraith**

Benjamin Franklin may have discovered electricity—but it was the man who invented the meter who made the money.
—**Earl Wilson**

Sudden money is going from zero to two hundred dollars a week. The rest doesn't count.
—**Neil Simon**

If women didn't exist, all the money in the world would have no meaning.
—**Aristotle Onassis**

Money is the most egalitarian force in society. It confers power on whoever holds it.
—**Roger Starr**

I've been rich, and I've been poor, and believe me, rich is better.
—**Joe E. Lewis**

Bankruptcy is a legal proceeding in which you put your money in your pants pocket and give your coat to your creditors.
—**Joey Adams**

Money demands that you sell, not your weakness to men's stupidity, but your talent to their reason.
—**Ayn Rand**

Half the world is composed of idiots, the other half of people clever enough to take indecent advantage of them.
—**Walter Kerr**

There were a few hustlers, who depended upon finding suckers for survival. And there were some who were too wise to hustle, who

only wanted to have enough money to be able to afford to be a sucker.
—**Duke Ellington**

The thermometer of success is merely the jealousy of the malcontents.
—**Salvador Dali**

The trouble with the rat race is that even if you win, you're still a rat.
—**Lily Tomlin**

People are not born bastards. They have to work at it.
—**Rod McKuen**

Slump, and the world slumps with you. Push and you push alone.
—**Laurence Peter**

Be awful nice to 'em going up, because you're gonna meet 'em all comin' down.
—**Jimmy Durante**

If you think the United States has stood still, who built the largest shopping center in the world?
—**Richard Nixon**

Nowadays people can be divided into three classes—the Haves, the Have-Nots, and the Have-Not-Paid-For-What-They-Haves.
—**Earl Wilson**

As far as unwed mothers on welfare are concerned, it seems to me they must be capable of some other form of labor.
—**Al Capp**

A lot of fellows nowadays have a B.A., M.D., or Ph.D. Unfortunately, they don't have a J.O.B.
—**Fats Domino**

A genius is one who can do anything except make a living.
—**Joey Adams**

Work is the curse of the drinking classes.
—**Mike Romanoff**

The better work men do is always done under stress and at great personal cost.
—**William Carlos Williams**

The world is full of willing people, some willing to work, the rest willing to let them.
—**Robert Frost**

An odd thing about New Orleans: The cemeteries here are more cheerful than the hotels and the French Quarter. Tell me why that should be, why 2,000 dead Creoles should be more alive than 2,000 Buick dealers?
—**Walker Percy**

Only a mediocre person is always at his best.
—**Laurence Peter**

When you're green, you're growing. When you're ripe, you rot.
—**Motto of Ray Kroc,** chairman of McDonald's

Success in almost any field depends more on energy and drive than it does on intelligence. This explains why we have so many stupid leaders.
—**Sloan Wilson**

I'm Freddie, fly me.
—**Freddie Laker**

Where all think alike, no one thinks very much.
—**Walter Lippmann**

Consultant: any ordinary guy more than fifty miles from home.
—**Eric Sevareid**

Specialist: a man who knows more and more about less and less.
—**Dr. William J. Mayo**

Make three correct guesses consecutively and you will establish a reputation as an expert.
—Laurence Peter

The real problem is what to do with the problem-solvers after the problems are solved.
—Gay Talese

Consultants are people who borrow your watch and tell you what time it is, and then walk off with the watch.
—Robert Townsend

Successful salesman: someone who has found a cure for the common cold shoulder.
—Robert Orben

If you sell diamonds, you cannot expect to have many customers. But a diamond is a diamond even if there are no customers.
—Swami Prabhupada

You know why Madison Avenue advertising has never done well in Harlem? We're not the only ones who know what it means to be Brand X.
—Dick Gregory

It is easier to make a businessman out of a musician than a musician out of a businessman.
—Goddard Lieberson

To have subsidized a Bach, or Fulbrighted a Beethoven would have done no good at all. Money may kindle but it cannot by itself, and for very long, burn.
—Igor Stravinsky

There's so much plastic in this culture that vinyl leopard skin is becoming an endangered synthetic.
—Lily Tomlin

Life is a series of yellow pads.
—George Stevens

The oilcan is mightier than the sword.
—**Everett Dirksen**

We are not so much running out of domestic oil as running out of
the oil companies' interest in looking for it.
—**Barry Commoner**

After perusing the world economic situation, we have come to the
conclusion to give you a break.
—**Shah Mohammed Riza Pahlevi of Iran,** indicating he would
   work to prevent further increases in oil prices, November 1977

Obviously, the answer to oil spills is to paper-train the
tankers.
—**Ralph Nader**

HARRY BENSON, PEOPLE WEEKLY © 1978 TIME INC.

The national bird of the United States should be the sparrow. Spar-
rows are proliferating all over the place, while the eagle is an
endangered species. I for one don't want my country symbolized by
a fierce loser.
—**Sloan Wilson**

Remember this: the house doesn't beat a player. It merely gives him the opportunity to beat himself!
—Nicholas ("Nick The Greek") Dandalos

If all else fails, immortality can always be assured by spectacular error.
—John Kenneth Galbraith

The secret of business is to know something that nobody else knows.
—Aristotle Onassis

When two men in business always agree, one of them is unnecessary.
—William Wrigley, Jr.

The way you get to be a celebrity is to get control of the people's playthings. It's a little like children and their toys. You do not become a celebrity by controlling the people's money, their banks, their raw materials.
—Aristotle Onassis

If you have a lemon, make lemonade.
—Howard Gossage

Leadership appears to be the art of getting others to want to do something you are convinced should be done.
—Vance Packard

The best way to launch an Italian restaurant is to have it raided because the Mafia eats there. Everybody knows they eat well.
—Mario Puzo

It is no secret that organized crime in America takes in over forty billion dollars a year. This is quite a profitable sum, especially when one considers that the Mafia spends very little for office supplies.
—Woody Allen

It requires a certain kind of mind to see beauty in a hamburger bun. Yet, is it any more unusual to find grace in the texture and softly curved silhouette of a bun than to reflect lovingly on . . . the arrangement of textures and colors in a butterfly's wing?
—**Ray Kroc,** chairman of McDonald's

Man cannot live by incompetence alone.
—**Laurence Peter**

3

Women

IT IS NEARLY twenty years now since Betty Friedan threw in the dishtowel and dropped out of suburbia to man the first feminist camp and lead frustrated housewives in their crusade for equal opportunity.

When the President's Commission on the Status of Women reported that, in 1965, women were earning only half the wages of men for equal positions of employment, feminists took up their pickets and launched the National Organization for Women (1966). On Mother's Day, 1967, they threw aprons at the White House. Soon after, fifty women, in an act of symbolic defiance, went for lunch at the Plaza Hotel's Oak Room—then reserved for men only. On August 26, 1970, the 50th anniversary of the constitutional amendment giving women the right to vote, Gloria Steinem, Bella Abzug, and Betty Friedan led militant feminists in a march down Fifth Avenue which culminated in an historic bra-burning. Two years later, Steinem took the movement one step further when she liberated the media with the publication of *Ms*. The two-career family was, *mirabile dictu*, a radical idea in July 1972.

The feminine mystique has succeeded in burying millions of American women alive.
—**Betty Friedan**

Once upon a time . . . a Liberated Woman was someone who had sex before marriage and a job afterward.
—**Gloria Steinem**

No scared housewife, I. I was flying.
—**Erica Jong**

A liberated woman is one who feels confident in herself, and is happy in what she is doing. She is a person who has a sense of self. . . . It all comes down to freedom of choice.
—**Betty Ford**

If I have to, I can do anything. I am strong; I am invincible; I am woman.
—**Helen Reddy**

I'm not radical—I'm just aware. I've come a long way, baby.
—**Billie Jean King**

There are two kinds of women: those who want power in the world, and those who want power in bed.
—**Jacqueline Kennedy Onassis**

No one is born a woman.
—**Simone de Beauvoir**

I never had to become a feminist; I was born liberated.
—**Grace Slick**

The emotional, sexual, and psychological stereotyping of females begins when the doctor says: "It's a girl."
—**Shirley Chisholm**

Anatomy is destiny.
—**Sigmund Freud**

Freud is the father of psychoanalysis. It has no mother.
—**Germaine Greer**

Boys will be boys these days and so, apparently, will girls.
—**Jane Howard**

We have lived through the era when happiness was a warm puppy, and the era when happiness was a dry martini, and now we have come to the era when happiness is "knowing what your uterus looks like."
—Nora Ephron

Women have childbearing equipment. For them to choose not to use the equipment is no more blocking what is instinctive than it is for a man who, muscles or no, chooses not to be a weightlifter.
—Betty Rollin

If men could get pregnant, abortion would be a sacrament.
—Florynce Kennedy

Love is the victim's response to the rapist.
—Ti-Grace Atkinson

All men are rapists and that's all they are. They rape us with their eyes, their laws, and their codes.
—Marilyn French

The stereotype is the Eternal Feminine. She is the Sexual Object sought by all men, and by all women. She is of neither sex, for she herself has no sex at all.
—Germaine Greer

The image of woman as we know it is an image created by men and fashioned to suit their needs.
—Kate Millett

You cannot be free if you are contained within a fiction.
—Julian Beck

I'm the most liberated woman in the world. Any woman can be liberated if she wants to be. First, she has to convince her husband.
—Martha Mitchell

Man is not the enemy here, but the fellow victim. The real enemy is women's denigration of themselves.
—Betty Friedan

To me the expression Ms. really means misery.
—**Phyllis Schlafly**

Sisterhood—the movement—is beautiful, but such ugliness comes out. Women know the problem, but how much will they pay?
—**Ti-Grace Atkinson**

I was the first woman to burn my bra—it took the fire department four days to put it out!
—**Dolly Parton**

I'm all for women's lib, but does the price of freedom have to be unemployment?
—**Faye Dunaway**

Women's Liberation is just a lot of foolishness. It's the men who are discriminated against. They can't bear children. And no one's likely to do anything about that.
—**Golda Meir**

The notion that the maternal wish and the activity of mothering are instinctive or biologically predestined is baloney.
—**Betty Rollin**

With animals you don't see the male caring for the offspring. . . . It's against nature. It is a woman's prerogative and duty, and a privilege.
—**Princess Grace of Monaco**

Most women would rather cuddle a baby than a typewriter or a machine.
—**Phyllis Schlafly**

No laborer in the world is expected to work for room, board, and love—except the housewife.
—**Letty Cottin Pogrebin**

The biggest sin is sitting on your ass.
—**Florynce Kennedy**

The one major obstacle for women in this business is that the more successful you get, the more you tend to intimidate the men around you whom you may want to get next to.
—**Bonnie Raitt**

Boys don't make passes at female smart-asses.
—**Letty Cottin Pogrebin**

As a woman, to be competitive is to be passive.
—**Marianne Partridge**

66

Sometimes we need to exclude men from our organizations in order for women to learn to work together. We need our own psychic turf.
—**Gloria Steinem**

UNITED PRESS INTERNATIONAL PHOTO

99

Men are never so tired and harassed as when they have to deal with a woman who wants a raise.
—**Michael Korda**

We will have equality when a female schlemiel moves ahead as fast as a male schlemiel.
—**Estelle Ramey,** president of the Association of Women in Science

It would be preposterously naïve to suggest that a B.A. can be made as attractive to girls as a marriage license.
—**Dr. Grayson Kirk,** president of Columbia University

I feel very angry when I think of brilliant, or even interesting women whose minds are wasted on a home. Better have an affair. It isn't so permanent and you keep your job.
—**John Kenneth Galbraith**

I'm having trouble managing the mansion. What I need is a wife.
—**Ella T. Grasso,** governor of Connecticut

It's very difficult to run an army if the general is in love with the sergeant.
—**Margaret Mead**

Margaret Mead wasn't much help. What did I have in common with all those savages?
—**Erica Jong**

I don't believe man is woman's natural enemy. Perhaps his lawyer is.
—**Shana Alexander**

Fighting is essentially a masculine idea; a woman's weapon is her tongue.
—**Hermione Gingold**

They say women talk too much. If you have worked in Congress you know that the filibuster was invented by men.
—**Clare Boothe Luce**

Frailty, thy name is no longer woman.
—**Victor Riesel**

Don't agonize. Organize.
—**Florynce Kennedy**

I'm a revolutionary—a revolutionary woman!
—**Jane Fonda**

American women are fools because they try to be everything to everybody.
—**Viva**

Emancipation means equal status for different roles.
—**Arianna Stassinopoulos**

We cannot reduce women to equality. Equality is a step down for most women.
—**Phyllis Schlafly**

God made man, and then said I can do better than that and made woman.
—**Adela Rogers St. John**

Human beings are not animals, and I do not want to see sex and sexual differences treated as casually and amorally as dogs and other beasts treat them. I believe this could happen under the ERA.
—**Ronald Reagan**

The people who are for the ERA do not believe in equal rights for the people who are against the ERA.
—**Phyllis Schlafly**

If I die, don't send flowers—just send three more states.
—**Liz Carpenter,** on the passage of the ERA

These are the most sexist women in the world, who cannot solve their own problems and want the government to do it for them.
—**Phyllis Schlafly**

How long can we live with a constitution that is ambiguous about equality for every citizen, when the simple addition of a few words will put things right?
—**Alan Alda**

Nobody outside of a baby carriage or a judge's chamber can believe in an unprejudiced point of view.
—**Lillian Hellman**

Male supremacy, like other political creeds, does not finally reside in physical strength but in acceptance of a value system which is not biological.
—**Kate Millett**

God made men stronger but not necessarily more intelligent. He gave women intuition and femininity. And, used properly, that combination easily jumbles the brain of any man I've ever met.
—**Farrah Fawcett-Majors**

Woman's virtue is man's greatest invention.
—**Cornelia Otis Skinner**

Through Elizabeth, I have been able to better understand the plight of working women. She has described to me in vivid detail how Louis B. Mayer shouted at her when she was ten.
—**John Warner**

I've been through it all, baby. I'm Mother Courage.
—**Elizabeth Taylor**

Work is not really new for women; what is new for women is the chance to be leaders.
—**Clay Felker**

Most hierarchies were established by men who now monopolize the upper levels, thus depriving women of their rightful share of opportunities for incompetence.
—**Laurence Peter**

You cannot decree women to be sexually free when they are not economically free.
—**Shere Hite**

Someday perhaps change will occur when times are ready for it instead of always when it is too late. Someday change will be accepted as life itself.
—**Shirley MacLaine**

Prostitution is . . . the very core of the female's social condition. . . . It is not sex the prostitute is really made to see: it is degradation.
—**Kate Millett**

One of the trump cards that men who are threatened by women's liberation are always dredging up is the question of whether there is sex after liberation.
—**Nora Ephron**

No gesture is more gallant than the courage to spit in the eye.
—**Shana Alexander**

Let it all hang out. Let it seem bitchy, catty, dykey, frustrated, crazy, Solanesque . . . nutty, frigid, ridiculous, bitter, embarrassing, man-hating, libelous, pure, unfair, envious, intuitive, lowdown, stupid, petty, liberating. We are the women that men have warned us about.
—**Robin Morgan**

There's a fine line between being sweet and innocent and being a tough broad.
—**Phyllis George**

A sharp knife cuts the quickest and hurts the least.
—**Katharine Hepburn**

Once you know what women are like, men get kind of boring. I'm not trying to put them down, I mean I like them sometimes as people, but sexually they're dull.
—**Rita Mae Brown**

The libs will learn that lesbian privileges and child care and the equal rights amendment and abortion are antifamily goals, and not what the American people want.
—**Phyllis Schlafly**

The great question that has never been answered, and which I have not yet been able to answer despite my thirty years of research into the feminine soul, is: What does a woman want?
—Sigmund Freud

It is a cliché of our time that women spent half a century fighting for "rights," and the next half wondering whether they wanted them after all.
—Betty Friedan

Women—the greatest undeveloped natural resource in the world today.
—Edward Steichen

To get it right, be born with luck or else make it. Never give up. A little money helps, but what really gets it right is to never . . . under any conditions face the facts.
—Ruth Gordon

I'm nobody's steady date. I can always be distracted by love, but eventually I get horny for my creativity.
—Gilda Radner

Freedom, especially a woman's freedom, is a conquest to be made, not a gift to be received. It isn't granted. It must be taken.
—Federico Fellini

The middle-class woman is now getting to the point where she thinks she has no choice because she thinks she has to do everything herself.
—Viva

We have a right to our own bodies.
—Shere Hite

Intercourse is an assertion of mastery, one that announces his own higher caste and proves it upon a victim who is expected to surrender, serve, and be satisfied.
—Kate Millett

My purpose in this book [Against Our Will: Men, Women, and Rape] has been to give rape its history. Now we must deny it a future.
—Susan Brownmiller

Sex is the only frontier open to women who have always lived within the confines of the feminine mystique.
—**Betty Friedan**

All too many men still seem to believe, in a rather naïve and ego-centric way, that what feels good to them is automatically what feels good to women.
—**Shere Hite**

To each masquerading male the female is a mirror in which he beholds himself.
—**Kate Millett**

I am a politician first, and a black and a woman second and third.
—**Barbara Jordan**

The myth of the strong black woman is the other side of the coin of the myth of the beautiful dumb blonde.
—**Eldridge Cleaver**

We are not going to abolish the family. We are not going to abolish marriage. We are not going to abolish the office. But we can change the structure.
—**Betty Friedan**

Free to be you and me.
—**Marlo Thomas**

Male and female are really two cultures and their life experiences are utterly different.
—**Kate Millett**

Most women still need a room of their own and the only way to find it may be outside their own homes.
—**Germaine Greer**

One can never consent to creep when one feels an impulse to soar.
—**Helen Keller**

a little zen in our politics a little acid in our tea, could be all we need. the poof is in the putting.
—**Jill Johnston**

There are men I could spend eternity with,
But not this life.
—**Kathleen Norris**

It was either Isaac Newton or maybe it was Wayne Newton who
once said, "A septic tank does not last forever." He was right.
—**Erma Bombeck**

A suburban mother's role is to deliver children obstetrically once,
and by car forever after.
—**Peter De Vries**

When men reach their sixties and retire, they go to pieces. Women
just go right on cooking.
—**Gail Sheehy**

What I am defending is the real rights of women. A woman should
have the right to be in the home as a wife and mother.
—**Phyllis Schlafly**

I can't be a rose in any man's lapel.
—**Margaret Trudeau**

Being a housewife and a mother is the biggest job in the world, but
if it doesn't interest you, don't do it. . . . I would have made a terrible parent. The first time my child didn't do what I wanted, I'd
kill him.
—**Katharine Hepburn**

Everybody's mother still cares.
—**Lillian Hellman**

A woman is her mother.
—**Anne Sexton**

Love is the only circumstance in which the female is (ideologically)
pardoned for sexual activity.
—**Kate Millett**

Like most women, most of what I knew about sex came from men.
—**Shere Hite**

Thoughts have no sex.
—**Clare Boothe Luce**

There is no such thing as homosexual or heterosexual. . . . We're so uptight about sensuality that the only people we can stroke as expressions of affection are children and dogs.
—**Kate Millett**

What's the point of being a lesbian if a woman is going to look and act like an imitation man?
—**Rita Mae Brown**

A transsexual loves women so much he wants to join them.
—**Dr. Renee Richards**

The journey that I've just completed seems to be the journey to end all journeys . . . from one side of humanity to the other.
—**James/Jan Morris**

The lesbian is an attorney, an architect, or an engineer. She is the blind poet and songwriter. She is a welfare recipient, an auto mechanic, a veterinarian, an alcoholic, a telephone operator, a civil service or civil rights worker. And, being a woman in Western society, she is certainly a clerk-typist, secretary, or bookkeeper.
—**Del Martin** and **Phyllis Lyon**

All human life on the planet is born of woman.
—**Adrienne Rich**

The woman is the fiber of the nation. She is the producer of life. A nation is only as good as its women.
—**Muhammad Ali**

I always introduce myself as . . . an encyclopedia of defects which I do not deny. Why should I? It took me a whole life to build myself as I am.
—**Oriana Fallaci**

The cross is just the true shape of a tortured woman.
—**Patti Smith**

I'd like to thank God, because She makes everything possible.
—**Helen Reddy,** accepting her Grammy award

The basic and essential human is the woman.
—**Orson Welles**

Woman is not completed reality, but rather a becoming.
—**Simone de Beauvoir**

Women are not inherently passive or peaceful. We're not inherently anything but human.
—**Robin Morgan**

Who knows what women can be when they are finally free to become themselves?
—**Betty Friedan**

4
Macho

IN APRIL 1972, Burt Reynolds posed the challenge to *Playboy*'s "Playmate of the Month" by becoming the first male nude centerfold of *Cosmopolitan*. Such exhibitions of virility, updating the ancient Hispanic code of *machismo*, gained even greater acceptance among the American public in 1978, when a rock group called "Village People" found their record "Macho Man" catapulted to the top of the charts.

I wanted to be called Mr. March.
—**Burt Reynolds,** on his nude centerfold for *Cosmopolitan*

Power is the ultimate aphrodisiac.
—**Henry Kissinger**

A great philosopher once said—I think it was Henry Kissinger—nobody will ever win the battle of the sexes. There's just too much fraternizing with the enemy.
—**Robert Orben**

Male chauvinism is . . . a shrewd method of extracting the maximum of work for the minimum of compensation.
—**Michael Korda**

Women in general want to be loved for what they are and men for what they accomplish.
—**Theodor Reik**

Si Non Oscillas Noli Tintinnare.
—**Hugh Hefner's sign** at the front door of Playboy Mansion. Translation: If you don't swing, don't ring.

Life begins at the centerfold and expands outward.
—**Lisa Baker,** Playmate of the Month, November 1966

If you got it, baby, flaunt it.
—**Mel Brooks**

I owe every woman in America an apology.
—**Larry Flynt,** publisher of *Hustler*

The only position for women in SNCC is prone.
—**Stokely Carmichael**

Men are beasts, and even beasts don't behave as they do.
—**Brigitte Bardot**

Women are a problem, but if you haven't already guessed, they're the kind of problem I enjoy wrestling with.
—**Warren Beatty**

Women would be the most enchanting creatures on earth if, in falling into their arms, one didn't fall into their hands.
—**Eddie Fisher**

For a woman to be loved, she usually ought to be naked.
—**Pierre Cardin**

There are only two kinds of women—goddesses and doormats.
—**Pablo Picasso**

Sex is one of the nine reasons for reincarnation. . . . The other eight are unimportant.
—**Henry Miller**

Sex is the cure-all.
—**Joe Namath**

Women? I guess they ought to exercise Pussy Power.
—**Eldridge Cleaver**

Chastity: the most unnatural of the sexual perversions.
—**Aldous Huxley**

Once they call you a Latin Lover, you're in real trouble. Women expect an Oscar performance in bed.
—**Marcello Mastroianni**

It's not the men in my life that counts—it's the life in my men.
—**Mae West**

There's nothing in the world you can do with a seventy-five-year-old woman but be nice to her.
—**Billy Carter**

I'm just naturally respectful of pretty girls in tight-fitting sweaters.
—**Jack Paar**

The men who really wield, retain, and covet power are the kind who answer bedside phones while making love.
—**Nicholas Pileggi**

The major civilizing force in the world is not religion, it's sex.
—**Hugh Hefner**

It's just as Christian to get down on your knees for sex as it is for religion.
—**Larry Flynt**

A woman's place is in the bedroom and the kitchen, in that order.
—**Bobby Riggs**

A woman's place . . . is in the bed or at the sink, and the extent of her travels should be from one to the other and back.
—**Caitlin Thomas**

They have a right to work wherever they want to—as long as they have dinner ready when you get home.
—**John Wayne,** on the liberated woman

All right, Edith, you go right ahead and do your thing . . . but just remember that your thing is eggs over-easy and crisp bacon.
—**Archie Bunker**

The best prescription for a discontented female is to have a child.
—**Pablo Picasso**

If you don't need any more babies, what do you need a family for?
—**Gore Vidal**

A woman's place is in the wrong.
—**James Thurber**

I don't drink or smoke. But I do chew gum, because Fu Man Chu.
—**Bruce Lee**

Probably the only place where a man can feel really secure is in a maximum security prison, except for the imminent threat of release.
—**Germaine Greer**

I would still rather score a touchdown than make love to the prettiest girl in the United States.
—**Paul Hornung**

When you win, nothing hurts.
—**Joe Namath**

All a writer has to do to get a woman is to say he's a writer. It's an aphrodisiac.
—**Saul Bellow**

If there hadn't been women we'd still be squatting in a cave eating raw meat, because we made civilization in order to impress our girlfriends.
—**Orson Welles**

Growing up does not mean to the American boy taking on the responsibilities and the trials of full sexual behavior. Growing up means wearing long pants like his elder brother, driving a car, earning money, having a job, being his own boss, and taking a girl to the movies.
—**Margaret Mead**

What is a man? A miserable little pile of secrets.
—**André Malraux**

The only thing that holds a marriage together is the husband bein' big enough to step back and see where his wife is wrong.
—**Archie Bunker**

If it were natural for fathers to care for their sons, they would not need so many laws commanding them to do so.
—**Phyllis Chesler**

Man isn't a noble savage; he's an ignoble savage.
—**Stanley Kubrick**

The myth of the noble savage is bull. People are born to survive.
—**Sam Peckinpah**

I do nothing that a man of unlimited funds, superb physical endurance, and maximum scientific knowledge could not do.
—**Batman**

On James Bond: He smoked like Peter Lorre and drank like Humphrey Bogart and ate like Sydney Greenstreet and used up girls like Errol Flynn and then went out to a steam bath and came out looking like Clark Gable. It was all so reassuring that we never stopped to think that all these people are dead.
—**Harry Reasoner**

A man will take any girl to bed, and it has nothing to do with any attraction for her or his love for his wife. A woman may like to think she is the same, that she is equal, but she's not, because when she loves her man, she'll be faithful to him. A woman's love for a man is greater than a man's love for a woman.
—**Tom Jones**

Male sexual response is far brisker and more automatic: it is triggered easily by things, like putting a quarter in a vending machine.
—**Alex Comfort, M.D.**

Men and women are quite different in temperament and needs, and the feminists' efforts to deny this is increasing the rivalry between the sexes and impairing the pleasure of both.
—**Dr. Benjamin Spock**

There's nothing so similar to one poodle dog as another poodle dog and that goes for women, too.
—**Pablo Picasso**

For a man there are three certainties in life: death, taxes, and women. It is often difficult to say which is the worst.
—**Dr. Albert Ellis**

Men are not given awards and promotions for bravery in intimacy.
—**Gail Sheehy**

Why can't a woman be more like a man?
—**Henry Higgins**

I sleep with men and with women. I am neither queer nor not queer, nor am I bisexual.
—**Allen Ginsberg**

There's nothing wrong with going to bed with somebody of your own sex. . . . People should be very free with sex—they should draw the line at goats.
—**Elton John**

The mind is an erogenous zone.
—**David Frost**

Being baldpate is an unfailing sex magnet.
—Telly Savalas

I may have faults but being wrong ain't one of them.
—Jimmy Hoffa

Macho does not prove mucho.
—Zsa Zsa Gabor

Never loan shylock money to a woman, because you can't beat her up to collect.
—Mafia motto

Mafia families do not consist of a wife and children who always go to places like the circus or on picnics. They are actually groups of rather serious men, whose main joy in life comes from seeing how long certain people can stay under the East River before they start gurgling.
—Woody Allen

The spur of the moment is the essence of adventure.
—Antony Armstrong-Jones

Freedom's just another word for nothing left to lose.
—Kris Kristofferson

Early to rise and early to bed makes a male healthy and wealthy and dead.
—James Thurber

I like men to behave like men—strong and childish.
—Françoise Sagan

Cool comes natural to me. Cool is the way I dress. Cool is the way I dribble.
—Walt Frazier

In the forties, to get a girl you had to be a GI or a jock. In the fifties, to get a girl you had to be Jewish. In the sixties, to get a girl you had to be black. In the seventies, to get a girl you've got to be a girl.
—Mort Sahl

I'd never seen men hold each other. I thought the only things they were allowed to do was shake hands or fight.
—**Rita Mae Brown**

When a man sits with a pretty girl for an hour, it seems like a minute. But let him sit on a hot stove for a minute—and it's longer than any hour. That's relativity.
—**Albert Einstein**

Men who are "orthodox" when they are young are in danger of being middle-aged all their lives.
—**Walter Lippmann**

The handsome, witty, charming men are the men for whom women give up their identities—they don't do it for killers.
—**Paul Mazursky**

66

Manhood at the most basic level can be validated and expressed only in action.
—**George Gilder**

WIDE WORLD PHOTOS

99

The difference between men and boys is the price of their toys.
—**Liberace**

The royal road to a man's heart is to talk to him about the things he treasures most.
—**Dale Carnegie**

The world's a cuckold from beginning to end.
—**Salvador Dali**

Honey, whatever women do, they do best after dark.
—**John Lindsay**

I know a great many women, and I have found each one to be not just a world apart, but a whole universe.
—**Yul Brynner**

The definition of a beautiful woman is one who loves me.
—**Sloan Wilson**

Sexiness in a woman is certainly a redeeming social value.
—**Peter Bogdanovich**

A man's sexual choice is the result and the sum of his fundamental convictions. Tell me what a man finds sexually attractive and I will tell you his entire philosophy of life.
—**Ayn Rand**

The most important thing a man can know is that, as he approaches his own door, someone on the other side is listening for the sound of his footsteps.
—**Clark Gable**

Man is not made for defeat.
—**Ernest Hemingway**

When I was young, I used to have successes with women because I was young. Now I have successes with women because I am old. Middle age was the hardest part.
—**Arthur Rubinstein**

The French are true romantics. They feel the only difference between a man of forty and one of seventy is thirty years of experience.
—**Maurice Chevalier**

If you cannot catch a bird of paradise, better take a wet hen.
—**Nikita Khrushchev**

Women are usually more patient in working at unexciting repetitive
tasks.
—**Dr. Benjamin Spock,** deleted passage from the 1946 edition of
The Common Sense Book of Baby and Child Care

Girls have an unfair advantage over men: if they can't get what they
want by being smart, they can get it by being dumb.
—**Yul Brynner**

There are three things men can do with women: love them, suffer
for them, or turn them into literature.
—**Stephen Stills**

No man does right by a woman at a party.
—**Harry Golden**

Decent clothes . . . a car, but what's it all about?
—**Michael Caine,** as Alfie, at the end of the 1966 film of the same
name

5
Space

ON OCTOBER 4, 1957, the Great Space Race got off the ground when the Soviets scheduled the first flight beyond the stratosphere—a fifteen-week orbit of Sputnik I. Americans, challenged to keep pace with the Russians, launched the historic Explorer I on January 31, 1958. Several months later, the National Aeronautics and Space Administration was formed. In 1961, President Kennedy committed the resources of this country to establishing a new frontier on the moon, setting a ten-year deadline on NASA's three-stage program to land an astronaut on the moon and return him to earth.

On July 20, 1969, more than a year ahead of schedule, Neil Armstrong walked on the moon for the television cameras. Millions of people actually tuned into outer space in living color. As a result of this mission accomplished, the Americans became the leading pioneers of the Space Age in the 1970s—currently scheduling shuttle flights from Cape Canaveral to outer space for female astronauts in the 1980s.

66

That's one small step for man, one giant leap for mankind.
—**Neil Armstrong,** the first man to set foot on the moon,
July 20, 1969

NASA

99

This is the greatest week in the history of the world since the Creation.
—**Richard Nixon,** July 20, 1969

We're Number One on the runway.
—**Neil Armstrong,** preparing to take off from the moon to return
to earth

Good-by, good night. Merry Christmas. God bless all of you, all of
you on the good earth.
—**Frank Borman,** Christmas Eve telecast from Apollo VIII, December 24, 1968

I'm the link between Ham the Space Chimp and Man.
—**Alan Shepard,** first American in space, after his May 5, 1961
flight

We're on top of the world. I'll tell you, you can't believe it . . . utterly fantastic. The world is round.
—**Charles (Pete) Conrad,** from Gemini XI

I don't know what you could say about a day in which you have seen four beautiful sunsets.
—**John Glenn,** the first American to orbit the earth, February 20, 1962

Beautiful, beautiful, beautiful. A magnificent desolation.
—**Edwin (Buzz) Aldrin,** the second man to set foot on the moon

There seems to be a lot of traffic up here. Call a policeman.
—**Walter (Wally) Schirra,** in Gemini VII while docking with Gemini VI, August 1, 1969

Four days vacation with pay and see the world.
—**James Lovell,** commenting on his Gemini XII mission

Sputnik doesn't worry me one iota. Apparently from what they say, they have put one small ball in the air.
—**Dwight D. Eisenhower,** 1957

I have never believed that a spectacular dash to the moon, vastly deepening our debt, is worth the added tax burden it will eventually impose upon our citizens.
—**Dwight D. Eisenhower,** 1963

There is just one thing I can promise you about the outer-space program: Your tax dollar will go farther.
—**Wernher von Braun**

I can't understand what's holding up our missile program. It's the first time the government ever had trouble making the taxpayer's money go up in smoke.
—**Bob Hope**

This nation has tossed its cap over the wall of space, and we have no choice but to follow it.
—**John F. Kennedy**

There is something more important than any ultimate weapon. That is the ultimate position—the position of total control over Earth that lies somewhere out in space.
—**Lyndon Baines Johnson**

For years, politicians have promised the moon. I'm the first one to be able to deliver it.
—Richard Nixon

In the nuclear age, by the time a threat has become unambiguous it may be too late to resist it.
—Henry Kissinger

The view of the moon is spectacular. Well worth the price.
—Neil Armstrong, from Apollo XI

Science cannot bear the thought that there is an important natural phenomenon which it cannot hope to explain even with unlimited time and money.
—Robert Jastrow

This nation should commit itself to achieving the goal, before the decade is out, of landing a man on the moon and returning him safely to earth.
—John F. Kennedy, May 25, 1961

According to information received from Cape Canaveral, a rocket with a man on board was launched. After fifteen minutes the capsule with the pilot, Alan Shepard, fell in the Atlantic Ocean.
—Soviet news release of the first United States manned flight

The Roman Empire controlled the world because it could build roads. . . . The British Empire was dominant because it had ships. In the air age, we were powerful because we had airplanes. Now the Communists have established a foothold in outer space. It is not very reassuring to be told that next year we will put a better satellite into the air. Perhaps it will even have chrome trim and automatic windshield wipers.
—Lyndon Baines Johnson

What we will have attained when Neil Armstrong steps down upon the moon is a completely new step in the evolution of man.
—Wernher von Braun

One of our problems is trying to figure out which way is up and which way is down.
—John Young, from Apollo X

Boy, this is beautiful. Boy oh boy. It looks that pretty. Boy oh boy.
—**Gordon Cooper,** the first astronaut to orbit in space, Mercury-
Atlas IX

Let them eat moon-shots!
—**Isaac Asimov,** updating Marie Antoinette

It suddenly struck me that that tiny pea, pretty and blue, was the
earth. I put up my thumb and shut one eye, and my thumb blotted
out the planet Earth. I didn't feel like a giant. I felt very, very small.
—**Neil Armstrong,** on the Apollo XI return trip

The only way to define the limits of the possible is by going beyond
them into the impossible.
—**Arthur C. Clarke**

No. No. I won't go! You can't make me!
—**Gordon Cooper,** showing newsmen what astronauts go
through before entering the capsule

I was a rotten S.O.B. before I left. Now I'm just an S.O.B.
—**Alan Shepard,** after becoming America's first astronaut

There is a single light of science, and to brighten it anywhere is to
brighten it everywhere.
—**Isaac Asimov**

The moon is a different thing to each one of us. It looks like a vast,
lonely, forbidding place, an expanse of nothing.
—**Frank Borman,** from Apollo VIII while orbiting the moon

The great tragedy of Science—the slaying of a beautiful hypothesis
by an ugly fact.
—**Aldous Huxley**

If we die, we want people to accept it. We are in a risky business,
and we hope that if anything happens to us it will not delay the
program. The conquest of space is worth the risk of life.
—**Virgil (Gus) Grissom,** astronaut killed in action on January 27,
1967

I'm like an orchestra conductor. I don't write the music, I just make sure it comes out right.
—**Christopher Kraft,** flight operation director of the Apollo missions

This has been far more than three men on a voyage to the moon. More even than the efforts of one nation. . . . This stands as a symbol of the insatiable curiosity of all mankind to explore the unknown.
—**Edwin (Buzz) Aldrin,** from Apollo XI shortly before splashdown

We are all on a spaceship and that spaceship is Earth. Four billion passengers—and no skippers.
—**Wernher von Braun**

I think Isaac Newton is doing most of the driving right now.
—**William A. Anders,** aboard Apollo VIII

I just don't think the moon is going to be an adequate substitute for the fact that we haven't addressed ourselves to clearing up the slums.
—**Kenneth B. Clark**

Basic research is what I am doing when I don't know what I am doing.
—**Wernher von Braun**

Any sufficiently advanced technology is indistinguishable from magic.
—**Arthur C. Clarke**

May the Force be with you.
—**Benediction of the good guys** in the film *Star Wars*

Somewhere, something incredible is waiting to be known.
—**Carl Sagan**

6
Liberation

EVER SINCE the integration of Central High School in Little Rock, Arkansas on September 24, 1957, the country has been invigorated by the spirit of liberation. The dream of equality which Dr. Martin Luther King, Jr. preached on the steps of the Lincoln Memorial in front of 250,000 demonstrators, on August 28, 1963, was shared by all oppressed groups—women, homosexuals, students, blacks, and senior citizens.

On July 2, 1964, President Lyndon Johnson set the tenor for the liberation movement of the 1960s by signing into law the most sweeping civil rights legislation in American history. As blacks laid claim to their equal rights, riots broke out across the country in Detroit, Newark, Rochester—and Watts. On April 4, 1968, Dr. King was assassinated in Memphis while supporting a civil sanitation workers strike.

On February 20, 1970 the Chicago Seven—Abbie Hoffman, Jerry Rubin, Tom Hayden, Rennie Davis, David Dellinger, Lee Weiner and John Froines—were found guilty of crossing state lines with intent to incite riots at the 1968 Democratic Convention. The trial marked the culmination of an era of political dissent, when youth and leftist activists charged politicians with the moral treason of hypocrisy.

There is a revolution coming. It will not be like revolutions of the past. It will originate with the individual and with culture, and it will . . . not require violence to succeed. . . . Its ultimate creation will be a new and enduring wholeness and beauty—a renewed relationship of man to himself, to other men, to society, to nature, and to the land.
—**Charles Reich**

By the end, everybody had a label—pig, liberal, radical, revolutionary. . . . If you had everything but a gun, you were a radical but not a revolutionary.
—**Jerry Rubin**

The first duty of a revolutionary is to get away with it.
—**Abbie Hoffman**

To be a revolutionary you have to be a human being. You have to care about people who have no power.
—**Jane Fonda**

The true revolutionary is guided by a great feeling of love.
—**Che Guevara**

We want to create a world in which love is more possible.
—**Carl Oglesby,** president of the Students for a Democratic
Society

I have a dream that one day . . . the sons of former slave-owners will be able to sit down together at the table of brotherhood.
—**Dr. Martin Luther King, Jr.,** the March on Washington, August 28, 1963

As I would not be a slave, so I would not be a master. Whatever differs from this, to the extent of the difference, is no democracy.
—**Barbara Jordan**

Revolution is the festival of the oppressed.
—**Germaine Greer**

Women must become revolutionary. This cannot be evolution but revolution.
—**Shirley Chisholm**

The only alliance I would make with the Women's Liberation Movement is in bed.
—**Abbie Hoffman**

You can jail a revolutionary, but you cannot jail the revolution.
—**Bobby Seale,** national chairman of the Black Panther Party

It's a sad and stupid thing to have to proclaim yourself a revolutionary just to be a decent man.
—**David Harris**

Who of us knows for sure a revolutionary when he sees one, even if it is himself?
—**Hortense Calisher**

66

Make love, not war.
—**San Francisco hippies** in Haight-Ashbury

WIDE WORLD PHOTOS

99

I am a person. Do not bend, fold, spindle, or mutilate.
—**Picket sign** at the Berkeley riots, 1964

American youth is looking for a reason to die.
—**Jerry Rubin**

I am a citizen of the American dream, and the revolutionary struggle of which I am a part is a struggle against the American nightmare.
—**Eldridge Cleaver**

Violence is as American as cherry pie.
—**Stokely Carmichael**

Today a doctor could make a million dollars if he could figure a way to bring a boy into the world without a trigger finger.
—**Arthur Miller**

Shoot to Live!
—**Slogan** for the Weathermen

The only thing that's been a worse flop than the organization of nonviolence has been the organization of violence.
—**Joan Baez**

We had a sense of importance that would have led us to risk our lives for our rhetoric.
—**Jerry Rubin**

I can live with the robber barons, but how do you live with these pathological radicals?
—**Daniel Patrick Moynihan**

We're not really pacifists, we're just nonviolent soldiers.
—**Joan Baez**

In any nonviolent campaign there are four basic steps: collection of the facts to determine whether injustices exist, negotiation, self-purification, and direct action.
—**Dr. Martin Luther King, Jr.**

We are all human be-ins.
—**Jerry Rubin**

I'm campaigning on behalf of human beings.
—**Jane Fonda**

I would like to nominate Academy Award-winning actress Jane Fonda for a new award: the rottenest, most miserable performance by any one individual American in the history of our country.
—**Robert H. Steele,** Representative from Connecticut

All reactionaries are paper tigers.
—**Mao Tse-tung**

A revolution is coming—a revolution which will be peaceful if we are wise enough; compassionate if we care enough; successful if we are fortunate enough—but a revolution which is coming whether we will it or not. We can affect its character; we cannot alter its inevitability.
—**Robert F. Kennedy**

A spirit of national masochism prevails, encouraged by an effete corps of impudent snobs who characterize themselves as intellectuals.
—**Spiro T. Agnew**

It wasn't a revolt against the campus; it was a revolt on campus against things that were happening in American society—including the war.
—**Clark Kerr**

Up against the wall, motherfuckers.
—**Students** at Columbia University, 1968

Academic freedom can get you killed.
—**Spiro T. Agnew**

If it takes a bloodbath, let's get it over with. No more appeasement.
—**Ronald Reagan,** on the question of silencing campus radicals
   in 1970

No one in his right mind would make such a statement.
—**Ronald Reagan's press secretary,** upon hearing this remark

When you've got a problem with swine, you've got to call in the pigs.
—**S. I. Hayakawa,** president of San Francisco State College in the 1960s

No one can blame the policeman. He is the way he is because Americans have never understood the Bill of Rights.
—**Gore Vidal**

We can learn more from any jail than we can from any university.
—**Students** at Berkeley during the 1964 riots

Nobody starved in the streets of Berkeley.
—**Jerry Rubin**

I have never seen a situation so dismal that a policeman couldn't make it worse.
—**Brendan Behan**

The new generation must make their revolution by the yeast theory; they must spread their life.
—**Charles Reich**

The first part of the Yippie program, you know, is kill your parents.
—**Jerry Rubin**

Until you're prepared to kill your parents, you're not really prepared to change the country because our parents are our first oppressors.
—**Jerry Rubin**

The young are generally full of revolt, and are often pretty revolting about it.
—**Mignon McLaughlin**

Action is the only reality; not only reality but morality as well.
—**Abbie Hoffman**

High school students are the largest oppressed minority in America.
—**Jerry Rubin**

We must not mistake noise for weight, anger for argument, militance for virtue, passion for sense, or gripes for principles.
—**Leo Rosten**

The most exciting things going on in America today are movements to change America.
—**Mario Savio**

If you want a symbolic gesture, don't burn the flag, wash it.
—**Norman Thomas**

We were in the act of discovering ourselves, not what we had been instructed to discover by the culture.
—**Michael McClure**

We tell ourselves we are a counterculture. And yet are we really so different from the culture against which we rebel?
—**Jon Landau**

Students would be much better off if they could take a stand against taking a stand.
—**David Riesman**

Build not burn.
—**Slogan** of the Students for a Democratic Society

How many of you sick people are from the Students for a Democratic Society?
—**Spiro T. Agnew**

I, for one, do not think homosexuality is the latest advance over heterosexuality on the scale of human evolution. Homosexuality is a

sickness, just as are baby-rape or wanting to become the head of General Motors.
—**Eldridge Cleaver**

The back seat produced the sexual revolution.
—**Jerry Rubin**

If God had meant to have homosexuals, he would have created Adam and Bruce.
—**Anita Bryant**

If God dislikes gays so much, how come he picked Michelangelo, a known homosexual, to paint the Sistine Chapel ceiling while assigning Anita to go on TV and push orange juice?
—**Mike Royko**

I love gay people. . . . But they are not a minority whose rights have to be protected. They are not like blacks, because black sticks. . . . If gays are granted rights, next we'll have to give rights to prostitutes and to people who sleep with Saint Bernards and to nail-biters.
—**Anita Bryant**

When the sexual energy of the people is liberated they will break the chains.
—**Julian Beck**

We've been brain-damaged by society. We are expected to be docile, serene, compliant. . . . The Gray Panthers are a rallying point for a group of people who are not willing to accept this stereotype.
—**Maggie Kuhn,** leader of the Gray Panthers

The object is for everyone to do their own thing, but the thing is to make one's thing the Revolution.
—**Eldridge Cleaver**

The Revolution . . . is a dictatorship of the exploited against the exploiters.
—**Fidel Castro**

Revolution is a trivial shift in the emphasis of suffering.
—**Tom Stoppard**

The fundamental principle is that no battle, combat, or skirmish is to be fought unless it will be won.
—**Che Guevara**

Revolutions do not take place in velvet boxes.
—**Carl Oglesby,** president of the Students for a Democratic Society

A revolution is not a dinner party, or writing an essay, or painting a picture, or doing embroidery; it cannot be so refined.
—**Mao Tse-tung**

In this Revolution no plans have been written for retreat.
—**Dr. Martin Luther King, Jr.**

A revolution does not march in a straight line. It wanders where it can, retreats before superior forces, advances wherever it has room, attacks whenever the enemy retreats or bluffs and, above all, is possessed of enormous patience.
—**Mao Tse-tung**

I didn't get my ideas from Mao, Lenin, or Ho. I got my ideas from the Lone Ranger.
—**Jerry Rubin**

Shoot to kill any arsonist or anyone with a Molotov cocktail in his hand in Chicago because they're potential murderers . . . and shoot to maim or cripple anyone looting any stores in our city.
—**Mayor Richard Daley's** instructions to the Chicago superintendent of police, during the 1968 riots

Our crime was that we were beginning to live a new and contagious life-style without official authorization. We were tried for being out of control.
—**Tom Hayden,** Chicago Seven defendant

When I appear in the Chicago courtroom, I want to be tried not because I support the National Liberation Front—which I do—but

because I have long hair. Nor because I support the Black Liberation Movement, but because I smoke dope.
—**Abbie Hoffman**

My life has come to nothing. I am not anything any more. You have destroyed me and everybody else. Put me in jail now, for God's sake, and get me out of this place.
—**William Kunstler,** to Judge Julius Hoffman, while waiting to receive his sentence of four years for contempt in his defense of the Chicago Seven

Look at the John Birch Society. Look at Hitler. The reactionaries are always better organizers.
—**Cesar Chavez**

There is no sense in your praying-in, or laying-in, or standing-in, or sitting-in. . . . If America is not stopped in its tracks it will destroy the world.
—**Imamu Amiri Baraka (LeRoi Jones)**

If any demonstrator ever lays down in front of my car, it'll be the last car he'll ever lay down in front of.
—**George Wallace**

The white man seems tone-deaf to the total orchestration of humanity.
—**Malcolm X**

Beware of Greeks bearing gifts, colored men looking for loans, and whites who understand the Negro.
—**Adam Clayton Powell**

Black people have organizations that fight for black power, and Jews look out for each other. But there isn't anyone except the Klan who will fight for the rights of white people.
—**Grand Wizard David Duke,** of the Ku Klux Klan

A Klaner (KKK) is a cat who gets out of bed in the middle of the night and takes his sheet with him.
—**Dick Gregory**

There is no white world, there is no white ethnic, any more than there is a white intelligence.
—**Frantz Fanon**

White politicians may . . . say with their lips what they know with their minds they would feel with their hearts.
—**Eldridge Cleaver**

Nigguhs hate whites, and whites hate nigguhs. Everybody knows that deep down.
—**George Wallace**

A great many people think they are thinking when they are really rearranging their prejudices.
—**Edward R. Murrow**

Segregation Now, Segregation Tomorrow, Segregation Forever.
—**George Wallace**

Segregation is the offspring of an illicit intercourse between injustice and immorality.
—**Dr. Martin Luther King, Jr.**

If you want to make beautiful music, you must play the black and the white notes together.
—**Richard Nixon**

There is no separate black path to power and fulfillment that does not have to interact with white roots.
—**Dr. Martin Luther King, Jr.**

The NAACP is a wonderful organization. Belong to it myself. But do you realize if tomorrow morning we had complete integration, all them cats would be outta work?
—**Dick Gregory**

I'm sick and tired of black and white people of good intent giving aspirin to a society that is dying of a cancerous disease.
—**Reverend Ralph D. Abernathy**

The most persistent of all the attractive illusions in our country may be that racism can be ended by one single blow.
—McGeorge Bundy

Black is Beautiful.
—Stokely Carmichael, Mississippi Civil Rights Rally, June 26, 1966

If any man claims the Negro should be content . . . let him say he would willingly change the color of his skin and go to live in the Negro section of a large city. Then and only then has he a right to such a claim.
—Robert F. Kennedy

A black person never leaves the ghetto.
—Sammy Davis, Jr.

Now the doors are open and segregation is dead, although I don't know when they're going to have the funeral.
—Martin Luther King, Sr., 1977

What we mean by integration is not to be with them [whites] but to have what they have.
—Julian Bond

I want to be the white man's brother, but not his brother-in-law.
—Dr. Martin Luther King, Jr.

Integration today means the man who "makes it," leaving his black brothers behind in the ghetto as fast as his new sports car will take him.
—Stokely Carmichael

I try to stay away from only one kind of person during Brotherhood Week—the one who believes in integrated washrooms, integrated classrooms, integrated dining rooms, but separated checks.
—Dick Gregory

To be a Negro in this country and to be relatively conscious is to be in rage almost all the time.
—James Baldwin

To like an individual because he's black is just as insulting as to dislike him because he isn't white.
—e. e. cummings

Man is not an object to be admired; man is a person to be regarded.
—Reverend Jesse Jackson

Man is not the sum of what he has but the totality of what he does not have, of what he might have.
—Jean-Paul Sartre

It's been a struggle for me because I had a chance to be white and I refused.
—Richard Pryor

There's no black and white, left and right, to me anymore. There's only up and down, and down is very close to the ground.
—Bob Dylan

A man can't ride your back unless it's bent.
—Dr. Martin Luther King, Jr.

Nobody will save us from us for us but us.
—Reverend Jesse Jackson

We say "All power to the people": Black Power for black people, White Power for White People, Brown Power for Brown People, Red Power for Red People, and X Power for any group we've left out.
—Eldridge Cleaver

We all live under the same sky, but we don't all have the same horizon.
—Konrad Adenauer

I happen to know quite a bit about the South. Spent twenty years there one night.
—Dick Gregory

Color is not human or personal reality; it is a political reality.
—James Baldwin

I am probably the only living American, black or white, who just doesn't give a damn.
—**Adam Clayton Powell**

I had to see what I could do in the place no one else would go.
Stokely Carmichael

I am in Birmingham because injustice is here.
—**Dr. Martin Luther King, Jr.**

This culture is one of resistance, but a resistance of desperation.
—**Angela Davis**

We shall overcome.
—**Dr. Martin Luther King, Jr.**

Freedom is never voluntarily given by the oppressor; it must be demanded by the oppressed.
—**Dr. Martin Luther King, Jr.**

Living as a fugitive means resisting hysteria, distinguishing between the creations of a frightened imagination and the real signs that the enemy is near.
—**Angela Davis**

I am alone with the masses. Waiting.
—**Mao Tse-tung**

I wonder if you can compare the freedom of the millionaire with that of the beggar or of the unemployed.
—**Fidel Castro**

A man who won't die for something is not fit to live.
—**Dr. Martin Luther King, Jr.**

Death is the only inescapable, unavoidable, sure thing. We are sentenced to die the day we're born.
—**Gary Mark Gilmore**

Death comes to everyone but it varies in its significance. To die for the reactionary is as light as a feather. But to die for the revolution is heavier than Mount Tai.
—**Mao Tse-tung**

Political power grows out of the barrel of a gun.
—**Mao Tse-tung**

You cannot run faster than a bullet.
—**Idi Amin**

We are advocates of the abolition of war; we do not want war; but war can only be abolished through war; and in order to get rid of the gun it is necessary to pick up the gun.
—**Official motto** of the Black Panther Party

Dogma is less useful than cow dung.
—**Mao Tse-tung**

The whole country is one vast insane asylum and they're letting the worst patients run the place.
—**Robert Welch,** founder of the John Birch Society

The fight is never about grapes or lettuce. It is always about people.
—**Cesar Chavez**

Ignorance and poverty are the best condiments for the great feast of the world, but the inexperienced and poor are never invited to it.
—**Anthony Burgess**

The darkest thing about Africa is America's ignorance of it.
—**Reverend James J. Robinson**

I'd feel complimented if you called me a fanatic. The only ones who make things change are fanatics. If you're not a fanatic around here, you can't cut it.
—**Cesar Chavez**

One man's terrorist is another man's freedom fighter.
—**Yonan Alexander,** director of the Institute for Studies in International Terrorism

The growers don't care about people, and they never will. Their improvements, their labor-saving devices are all for their own benefit, not for ours.
—**Cesar Chavez**

A riot is the language of the unheard.
—**Dr. Martin Luther King, Jr.**

All we want is that we get our story told, and get it told right! What we do last night, maybe it wasn't right. But ain't nobody come down here and listen to us before.
—**Rioter** in Watts, August 11–21, 1965

Perhaps it would be possible for the Negro to become reconciled to his plight if he could be made to believe that his sufferings were for some remote, high sacrificial end; but sharing the culture that condemns him, and seeing that a lust for trash is what blinds the nation to his claims, is what sets storms rolling in his soul.
—**Richard Wright**

We shall see who emerges from the labyrinth: the minotaur or the man.
—**Daniel Berrigan**

In 1966 I was arrested in Paterson and railroaded into Trenton State Prison for a crime that I did not and could not have committed.
—**Jerry Rubin (Hurricane) Carter**

Down South they don't care how close I get as long as I don't get too big; and up North they don't care how big I get as long as I don't get too close.
—**Dick Gregory**

They wouldn't have me in a maximum security prison if I wasn't interested in getting out.
—**James Earl Ray**

I died in that fire on 54th Street, but out of the ashes I was reborn.
—**Patricia (Tanya) Hearst**

It's just too bad we can't have an epidemic of botulism.
—**Ronald Reagan,** on the Symbionese Liberation Army's demand for food for the poor in exchange for the release of Patricia Hearst

I was coerced.
—**Patricia Hearst**

In no sense do I advocate evading or defying the law . . . That would lead to anarchy. . . . An individual who breaks a law that conscience tells him is unjust, and who willingly accepts the penalty of imprisonment in order to arouse the conscience of the community over its injustice, is in reality expressing the highest respect for law.
—**Dr. Martin Luther King, Jr.**

We are a feelingless people. If we could really feel, the pain would be so great that we would stop all the suffering.
—**Julian Beck**

We've gone too far to turn back now. We must now let them know that nothing can stop it—not even death itself. We must be ready for a season of suffering.
—**Dr. Martin Luther King, Jr.**

Whenever death may surprise us, let it be welcome if our battle cry has reached even one receptive ear and another hand reaches out to take up our arms.
—**Che Guevara**

It really doesn't matter with me now because I've been to the mountaintop. Like anybody I would like to *live* a long life. Longevity has its place. But I'm not concerned about that now, I just want to do God's *will*. And he's allowed me to go up to the mountain, and I've looked over and I've seen the Promised Land.
—**Dr. Martin Luther King, Jr.**

Oh, my friend, it's not what they take away from you that counts—it's what you do with what you have left.
—**Hubert Humphrey**

> Free at last, free at last. Thank God Almighty, I'm free at last.
> —**Inscription** on the gravestone of Dr. Martin Luther King, Jr.

WIDE WORLD PHOTOS

You can kill a man but you can't kill an idea.
—**Medgar Evers**

7
LBJ

ON NOVEMBER 22, 1963, the day of the assassination of John F. Kennedy, Lyndon Baines Johnson was sworn in as the thirty-sixth president of the United States.

For the next five years and fifty-nine days, Johnson struggled to realize his promise of a Great Society. Though he was cast as a peace candidate in 1964, when he won a (then) all-time high percentage (61 percent) of the popular vote, and was recognized as a tough politician and a staunch supporter of civil rights, Johnson was shot down politically by his escalation of the bombing and failure to end the war in Vietnam.

In 1968, Johnson passed his candidacy to Hubert Humphrey, his vice president and a politician less reviled by the antiwar movement. He pulled on his boots and, with Lady Bird and his beagles, returned to the 360-acre Johnson ranch in Texas, where he died quietly on January 22, 1973.

Politics is the art of the possible.
—**Lyndon Baines Johnson**

This nation, this generation, in this hour, has man's first chance to build a Great Society, a place where the meaning of man's life matches the marvels of man's labor.
—**Lyndon Baines Johnson**

> " What the man in the street wants is not a big debate on fundamental issues; he wants a little medical care, a rug on the floor, a picture on the wall, a little music in the house, and a place to take Molly and the grandchildren when he retires.
> —**Lyndon Baines Johnson**
>
>
>
> UNITED PRESS INTERNATIONAL PHOTO "

This administration, today, here and now, declares unconditional war on poverty in America.
—**Lyndon Baines Johnson,** August 20, 1960

First, Ah'm gonna give you a two-minute lecture on integrity, and then Ah'm gonna ruin you.
—**Lyndon Baines Johnson,** to a Texas politician

I never trust a man unless I've got his pecker in my pocket.
—**Lyndon Baines Johnson**

A man without a vote is a man without protection.
—**Lyndon Baines Johnson**

The First Lady is an unpaid public servant elected by one person: her husband.
—**Lady Bird Johnson**

One lesson you'd better learn if you want to be in politics is that you never go out on a golf course and beat the president.
—**Lyndon Baines Johnson**

Presidents quickly realize that while a single act might destroy the world they live in, no one single decision can make life suddenly better or can turn history around for good.
—**Lyndon Baines Johnson**

I give these toothbrushes to friends, for then I know that from now until the end of their days, they will think of me the first thing in the morning, and the last at night.
—**Lyndon Baines Johnson**

You never want to give a man a present when he's feeling good.
—**Lyndon Baines Johnson**

What convinces is conviction.
—**Lyndon Baines Johnson**

I don't push worth a damn.
—**Lyndon Baines Johnson**

You ain't learnin' nothin' when you're talkin'.
—**Lyndon Baines Johnson**

To hunger for use and to go unused is the worst hunger of all.
—**Lyndon Baines Johnson**

Politics is action but it is not civil war. Civil war only comes when truth is forgotten.
—**Lyndon Baines Johnson**

A politician who can't feel a situation without having diagrams drawn up for him is no kind of politician.
—**Lyndon Baines Johnson**

A president's hardest task is not to *do* what is right but to *know* what is right.
—**Lyndon Baines Johnson**

There is but one way for a president to deal with the Congress, and that is continuously, incessantly, and without interruption. If it's really going to work, the relationship between the president and the Congress has got to be almost incestuous.
—**Lyndon Baines Johnson**

Government is an expression of philosophy, and active governments are inevitably guided by philosophers.
—**Lyndon Baines Johnson**

Even when President Johnson is announcing good news, it sounds like bad news. Vice President Humphrey should announce the bad news, because even when he is announcing bad news, it sounds like good news.
—**Art Buchwald**

Today our problem is not making miracles—but managing them.
—**Lyndon Baines Johnson**

I am going to build the kind of nation that President Roosevelt hoped for, President Truman worked for, and President Kennedy died for.
—**Lyndon Baines Johnson**

8
Vietnam

It was the battle cry of the civilians which escalated the Vietnam War into a grave moral crisis on the American home front. On March 6, 1965, the first American soldier *officially* set foot on Vietnamese soil. Two years later, on October 21, 1967, an infantry of citizen protesters stormed the Pentagon. By 1969, the antiwar movement had organized into an army of conscience which marched on Washington to confront the White House. (President Nixon was too engrossed in the Ohio State-Purdue football game on TV to take "time out" for his political opponents.)

On August 11, 1975, after 46,079 American casualties, the last American soldier left Vietnam, ending the longest war in U.S. history.

Bombs are falling on Vietnam, but it is an American tragedy.
—Jane Fonda

The draft is white people sending black people to fight yellow people to protect the country they stole from red people.
—**Line** from the rock musical *Hair*

The military don't start wars. Politicians start wars.
—**General William Westmoreland**

It doesn't require any particular bravery to stand on the floor of the Senate and urge our boys in Vietnam to fight harder, and if this war mushrooms into a major conflict and a hundred thousand young Americans are killed, it won't be U.S. Senators who die. It will be American soldiers who are too young to qualify for the Senate.
—**George McGovern,** to Everett Dirksen of Illinois, in the Senate, June 1966

We are going to have peace even if we have to fight for it.
—**Dwight D. Eisenhower**

The United States is determined to help Vietnam preserve its independence, protect its people against communist assassins, and build a better life.
—**John F. Kennedy,** in a letter to Vietnamese President Diem

We did not choose to be the guardians at the gate. But there is no one else.
—**Lyndon Baines Johnson**

We don't declare war any more; we declare national defense.
—**Eugene McCarthy**

I'm not going to be the first American president who loses a war.
—**Richard Nixon,** September 1969

We should go in and win—or else get out.
—**Russell Long**

We are not going to send American boys nine or ten thousand miles away from home to do what Asian boys ought to be doing for themselves.
—**Lyndon Baines Johnson,** October 21, 1964

The American soldier is here to build as well as kill.
—**General William Westmoreland,** October 18, 1966

My feeling is that you could kill every Viet Cong and North Vietnamese in South Vietnam and still lose the war.
—**General Wallace Green,** former commandant of the Marine Corps

"

What is the use of physicians like myself trying to help parents to bring up children healthy and happy, to have them killed in such numbers for a cause that is ignoble?
—**Dr. Benjamin Spock**

UNITED PRESS INTERNATIONAL PHOTO

"

Let the sun shine in.
—**Antiwar poster**

If we open the window, not only sunlight but many bad things will fly in.
—**Madame Ngo Dinh Nhu**

The only language that Hanoi understands is the language of force.
—**General William Westmoreland**

War is not healthy for children and other living things.
—Antiwar poster

The Vietnam war is totally abominable and illegal, and I'll continue
to oppose it by talking and engaging in peace and political activi-
ties. I feel a free soul, and if I'm in jail I'll still feel a free soul.
—Dr. Benjamin Spock, to the American Civil Liberties Union
    Legal Defense, upon his release on bail

Ten years in prison is very cheap if that would contribute to ending
this war.
—Daniel Ellsberg

To demonstrate is the easy thing. It is much harder to stay at home
and quietly work for peace.
—George McGovern

A political man can have as his aim the realization of freedom, but
he has no means to realize it other than through violence.
—Jean-Paul Sartre

The basic decision in Southeast Asia is . . . we must decide
whether to help these countries to the best of our ability or throw in
the towel and pull back our defenses to San Francisco. . . . We
would say to the world in this case that we don't live up to our trea-
ties and don't stand by our friends. This is not my concept. I recom-
mend that we move forward promptly with a major effort to help
these countries defend themselves.
—Lyndon Baines Johnson, May 1961

We are here because we made a promise. We have made other
promises in other parts of the world. If Moscow or Peking ever discover that the promises of the United States do not mean what they
say, then this world goes up in smoke.
—Dean Rusk, October 1966, after a trip to Vietnam

People who dismiss the domino theory are all wet.
—General William Westmoreland

I'm going to Vietnam at the request of the White House. President
Johnson says a war isn't really a war without my jokes.
—Bob Hope

The Establishment center . . . has led us into the stupidest and cruelest war in all history. That war is a moral and political disaster—a terrible cancer eating away the soul of the nation.
—George McGovern

The survival of an independent government in South Vietnam is so important to the security of all Southeast Asia and to the free world that I can conceive of no alternative other than to take all necessary measures within our capacity to prevent a Communist victory.
—Robert McNamara

One of the greatest casualties of the war in Vietnam is the Great Society . . . shot down on the battlefield of Vietnam.
—Dr. Martin Luther King, Jr.

Out of this war are going to come some of the finest people this country has ever seen.
—General William Westmoreland

Yippies, Hippies, Yahoos, Black Panthers, lions and tigers alike—I would swap the whole damn zoo for the kind of young Americans I saw in Vietnam.
—Spiro T. Agnew

You always write its's bombing, bombing, bombing. It's not bombing. It's air support.
—Colonel H. E. Opfer, air attaché at the United States embassy in Pnom-Penh

In the White House by day we knew Henry Kissinger as "the hawk of hawks." But in the evenings, a magical transformation took place. Touching glasses at a party with his liberal friends, the belligerent Kissinger would suddenly become a dove.
—H. R. Haldeman

You said that only God knew the answer to Vietnam. I regard that as an attack on my competence.
—Senator Wayne Morse, to Senator Philip Hart

I'm fed up to the ears with old men dreaming up wars for young men to die in.
—**George McGovern,** in rebuttal to Mississippi Senator John Stennis's suggestion that GIs might have to return to Cambodia

A commander must learn to live with frustration, interference, irritation, disappointment, and criticism, as long as he can be sure they do not contribute to failure.
—**General William Westmoreland**

All wars are popular for the first thirty days.
—**Arthur Schlesinger, Jr.**

Wars have never hurt anybody except the people who die.
—**Salvador Dali**

I want this nation we all love to turn away from cursing and hatred and war to the blessings of hope and brotherhood and love.
—**George McGovern**

I found draft resisters very conscientious, reasonable, and not fanatics. . . . They just seemed to feel that they could not collaborate in the war, and were prepared to go to prison.
—**Daniel Ellsberg**

We are here as American patriots, young and old, to build a country, to build a world that seeks the ways of peace—that teaches war no more. We meet today to reaffirm those ageless values that gave us birth—"life, liberty, and the pursuit of happiness." We meet to declare peace—to put an end to war, not in some vanishing future, but to end it *now*.
—**Antiwar speech** given in front of a crowd of 350,000 at the Washington Monument, November 1969

We need to devise a system within which peace will be more rewarding than war.
—**Margaret Mead**

The lesson to be learned from Vietnam is that we must get in earlier, be shrewder, and force the other side to practice the self-deception.
—**David Halberstam**

I do not believe that the men who served in uniform in Vietnam have been given the credit they deserve. It was a difficult war against an unorthodox enemy.
—**General William Westmoreland**

15,000 young Americans have been killed since Richard Nixon took office, and their blood is on his hands.
—**George McGovern**

I bring you Peace with Honor, not Peace with Surrender.
—**Richard Nixon,** on Vietnam, 1960.

9
Kent State

As KENT STATE UNIVERSITY students shuffled between classes at the noon hour on May 4, 1970, the campus suddenly erupted into a battlefield. National Guardsmen, summoned to the campus by Ohio Governor James A. Rhodes, had opened fire on a group of students peacefully demonstrating against the war in Cambodia. When the tear gas finally cleared, bodies lay bleeding: four students were found brutally shot to death—on American soil.

Kent went through the whole history of the student movement in four days.
—**Radical Student,** at Kent State

The actions of some students were violent and criminal, and those of some others were dangerous, reckless, and irresponsible. The indiscriminate firing of rifles into a crowd of students and the deaths that followed were unnecessary, unwarranted, and inexcusable.
—**The President's Commission** on Campus Unrest, October 1970

87

> My God! My God! They're killing us.
> —**Ron Steele,** Kent State freshman

WIDE WORLD PHOTOS

I felt like I'd just had an order to clean up a latrine. You do what you're told to do.
—**National Guardsman**

If these anarchists get away with it here, no campus in the country is safe.
—**Kent resident**

We hold the guardsmen, acting under orders and under severe psychological pressures, less responsible for the massacre than are Governor Rhodes and Adjutant General Del Corso, whose inflammatory statements produced these pressures.
—**Verdict** of 1,000 Kent State faculty members

I was just at the wrong place at the wrong time.
—**Dean Kahler**, paralyzed victim of the shooting

The martyrs at Kent State were the kids in National Guard uniforms.
—**Al Capp**

You mean you can get away with murder in this country?
—**Bernard Miller**, whose son Jeffrey was killed

The academic community is not to be considered a sanctuary for those who wish to disobey our laws. . . . But neither is the academic community a place where ideas—no matter how offensive—are to be suppressed.
—**Robert I. White**, president of Kent State University

It's about time we showed the bastards who's in charge.
—**National Guardsman**

A time to weep. A time to mourn. This is the time.
—**Captain William Reinhard** to a young National Guard rifleman

We have some reason to believe that the claim by the National Guard that their lives were endangered by the students was fabricated subsequent to the event.
—**The Justice Department**, October 1970

I have lost faith in justice in America.
—**Martin Scheuler**, whose daughter Sandy was killed

10
Couples

As the romanticism of the 1960s ebbed into the liberated 1970s, monogamy was clearly becoming passé. Masters and Johnson taught married couples human sexual response in trendy clinics—with run-on waiting lists. David M. Reuben instructed the house-wife on the joys of natural orgasm. By 1969, one out of every two weddings was headed for divorce—or the more creative alternative of open marriage. George and Nena O'Neill conceived marriage as a cohabitational experiment where only one question still remained: if husband and wife were both out on their respective dates, who was keeping an eye on the children?

Love means never having to say you're sorry.
—Erich Segal

Love never makes demands. Love is unconditional acceptance of him and his feelings.
—Marabel Morgan

Love . . . is mutuality of devotion forever subduing the antago-nisms inherent in divided functions.
—Erik Erikson

Love does not begin and end the way we seem to think it does. Love is a battle, love is a war; love is a growing up.
—**James Baldwin**

People think love is an emotion. Love is good sense.
—**Ken Kesey**

Love is like a friendship caught on fire. In the beginning a flame, very pretty, often hot and fierce but still only light and flickering. As love grows older, our hearts mature and our love becomes as coals, deep-burning and unquenchable.
—**Bruce Lee**

If love is the answer, could you rephrase the question?
—**Lily Tomlin**

The most exciting attractions are between two opposites that never meet.
—**Andy Warhol**

I go out with actresses because I'm not apt to marry one.
—**Henry Kissinger,** 1972

Henry's idea of sex is to slow the car down to thirty miles an hour when he drops you off at the door.
—**Barbara Howar,** on Henry Kissinger

Put together, narcissistic people can provide considerable misery for each other and an interesting evening for others.
—**Theodore Isaac Rubin**

Men are always ready to respect anything that bores them.
—**Marilyn Monroe**

Familiarity, truly cultivated, can breed love.
—**Dr. Joyce Brothers**

Eddie Fisher married to Elizabeth Taylor is like me trying to wash the Empire State Building with a bar of soap.
—**Don Rickles**

My folks met on the subway trying to pick each other's pockets.
—**Freddie Prinze**

My most fervent wish is that I shall meet a man who loves me for myself and not my money.
—**Christina Onassis**

Giving is the highest expression of potency.
—**Erich Fromm**

I have never hated a man enough to give his diamonds back.
—**Zsa Zsa Gabor**

A woman without a man is like a fish without a bicycle.
—**Gloria Steinem**

My wife's final decision seldom tallies with the one immediately following it.
—**Paul Newman**

Falling madly in love with someone is not necessarily the starting point to getting married.
—**Prince Charles**

Love is so much better when you are not married.
—**Maria Callas**

Although today there are many trial marriages . . . there is no such thing as a trial child.
—**Gail Sheehy**

Open marriage means an honest and open relationship between two people, based on the equal freedom and identity of both partners.
—**George** and **Nena O'Neill**

Open marriage is nature's way of telling you you need a divorce.
—**Marshall Brickman**

I haven't known any open marriages, though quite a few have been ajar.
—**Bob Hope**

Most marriages don't add two people together. They subtract one from the other.
—**James Bond,** in *Diamonds Are Forever*

I had a friend who was getting married. I gave her a subscription to *Modern Bride*. The subscription lasted longer than the marriage.
—**Lily Tomlin**

The run-of-the-mill have a truer capacity for love than intellectuals, who should know better.
—**Ned Rorem**

Without love intelligence is dangerous; without intelligence love is not enough.
—**Ashley Montagu**

Jacqueline Onassis has a very clear understanding of marriage. I have a lot of respect for women who win the game with rules given you by the enemy.
—**Gloria Steinem**

In any relationship in which two people become one, the end result is two half people.
—**Wayne Dyer**

I would rather be alone than be two people and still alone.
—**Genevieve Bujold**

The surest way to be alone is to get married.
—**Gloria Steinem**

I used to believe that anything was better than nothing. Now I know that sometimes nothing is better.
—**Glenda Jackson**

In love the paradox occurs that two beings become one and yet remain two.
—**Erich Fromm**

Marriage makes you legally half a person, and what man wants to live with half a person?
—**Gloria Steinem**

When two people marry they become in the eyes of the law one person, and that one person is the husband!
—Shana Alexander

To the average male there is seemingly nothing so attractive or so challenging as a reasonably good-looking young mother who is married and *alone*.
—Shirley MacLaine

Solitude is un-American.
—Erica Jong

To fear love is to fear life, and those who fear life are already three parts dead.
—Bertrand Russell

The only abnormality is the incapacity to love.
—Anaïs Nin

You shouldn't have to buy marriage off the rack; it should conform exactly to the contours of those who chose to clothe themselves in it.
—George and Nena O'Neill

Marriage is like a three-speed gearbox: affection, friendship, love. It is not advisable to crash your gears and go right through to love straightaway. You need to ease your way through. The basis of love is respect, and that needs to be learned from affection and friendship.
—Peter Ustinov

Friendship is everything. Friendship is more than talent. It is more than government. It is almost the equal of family.
—Line from *The Godfather*

Friendship is the hardest thing in the world to explain. It's not something you learn in school. But if you haven't learned the meaning of friendship, you really haven't learned anything.
—Muhammad Ali

Homosexuals make the best friends because they care about you as a woman and are not jealous. They love you but don't try to screw up your head.
—**Bianca Jagger**

The greatest healing therapy is friendship and love.
—**Hubert Humphrey**

We found that living together was getting in the way of our relationship. It doesn't mean we don't dig each other. It just means we can't live together.
—**David Harris,** Joan Baez's husband

We sleep in separate rooms, we have dinner apart, we take separate vacations—we're doing everything we can to keep our marriage together.
—**Rodney Dangerfield**

Having two bathrooms ruined the capacity to cooperate.
—**Margaret Mead**

A man's home is his hassle.
—**Paul D. Arnold**

I sleep well when Bella is in Washington. I sleep even better when she's in Cambodia.
—**Martin Abzug**

Your experience will be a lesson to all of us men to be careful not to marry ladies in very high positions.
—**Idi Amin,** to Lord Snowdon about the break-up of his marriage to Princess Margaret

You take my wife. Please.
—**Henny Youngman**

I am a marvelous housekeeper. Every time I leave a man, I keep his house.
—**Zsa Zsa Gabor**

Some married couples say, why don't we try twin beds instead of a double bed? We just went a little further and said, "Let's live in separate houses."
—**William Proxmire**

Sometimes I wonder if men and women really suit each other. Perhaps they should live next door and just visit now and then.
—**Katharine Hepburn**

A successful marriage is not a gift; it is an achievement.
—**Ann Landers**

I have learned only two things are necessary to keep one's wife happy. First, let her think she is having her own way. Second, let her have it.
—**Antony Armstrong-Jones**

Marriage isn't an up or down issue. . . . . It's a side-by-side one.
—**Prince Charles**

Love is the best, most insidious, most effective instrument of social repression.
—**Rainer Werner Fassbinder**

The best of all possible marriages is a seesaw in which first one, then the other partner is dominant.
—**Dr. Joyce Brothers**

Male domination has had some very unfortunate effects. It made the most intimate of human relations, that of marriage, one of master and slave, instead of between equal partners.
—**Bertrand Russell**

Mummy is the head of state, and I am boss in the house.
—**Prince Bernhard**

A strong man doesn't have to be dominant toward a woman. He doesn't match his strength against a woman weak with love for him. He matches it against the world.
—**Marilyn Monroe**

66

I always run into strong women who are looking for weak men to dominate them.
—**Andy Warhol**

WIDE WORLD PHOTOS

99

Today when a woman says "I do," that's the last thing she does.
—**Jackie Mason**

Marriage is the alliance of two people, one of whom never remembers birthdays and the other never forgets them.
—**Ogden Nash**

Love at eighteen is largely an attempt to find out who we are by listening to our echoes in the words of another.
—**Gail Sheehy**

Immature love says: "I love you because I need you." Mature love says: "I need you because I love you."
—**Erich Fromm**

They're not going to get married or anything. They're only nine.
—**Lillian Carter**, on Amy's first boyfriend

I am a woman meant for a man, but I never found a man who could compete.
—**Bette Davis**

You are a foul ball in the line drive of life.
—**Lucy**, to Charlie Brown

It takes two to destroy a marriage.
—**Margaret Trudeau**

It all comes down to who does the dishes.
—**Norman Mailer**

Marriage is the best magician there is. In front of your eyes, it can change an exciting cute little dish into a boring dishwasher.
—**Ryan O'Neal**

Marriage is like panty-hose. It all depends on what you put into it.
—**Phyllis Schlafly**

Marrying a man is like buying something you've been admiring for a long time in a shop window. You may love it when you get home, but it doesn't always go with everything else in the house.
—**Jean Kerr**

When I wake up in the morning, I think of *me* first and then my wife and then my children. I'd like to meet the guy that can honestly admit he does differently.
—**Jerry Lewis**

You never really know a man until you have divorced him.
—**Zsa Zsa Gabor**

After twenty years of marriage I don't know how to handle men yet.
—**Pat Loud**

Marriage essentially is a contract, and there are so many loopholes in it that Wilbur Mills and the entire Ways and Means Committee at their height couldn't figure it out.
—Warren Beatty

The difference between divorce and legal separation is that a legal separation gives a husband time to hide his money.
—Johnny Carson

No one ever filed for divorce on a full stomach.
—Mamma Leone

Even though a girl may loathe cooking, she should make an effort to cater to her husband's likes and dislikes and to make meals appetizing and interesting.
—Elizabeth Post

There is one thing more exasperating than a wife who can cook and won't, and that's the wife who can't cook and will.
—Robert Frost

The housewife is interested in serious things. It gives her something to tell her husband when he comes home.
—Mike Douglas

When I can no longer bear to think of the victims of broken homes, I begin to think of the victims of intact ones.
—Peter De Vries

I never loved another person the way I loved myself.
—Mae West

In an age when the fashion is to be in love with yourself, confessing to being in love with somebody else is an admission of unfaithfulness to one's beloved.
—Russell Baker

Marriages are like diets. They can be ruined by having a little dish on the side.
—Earl Wilson

I prefer the word "homemaker," because "housewife" always implies that there may be a wife someplace else.
—Bella Abzug

Husbands are chiefly good lovers when they are betraying their wives.
—Marilyn Monroe

My wife's jealousy is getting ridiculous. The other day she looked at my calendar and demanded to know who May was.
—Rodney Dangerfield

I am his mistress. His work is his wife.
—Marion Javits, wife of Senator Jacob Javits

Marriage is a half step, a way to leave home without losing home.
—Gail Sheehy

By the act of marriage you endorse all the ancient and dead values. You endorse things like monogamy. Lifelong monogamy is a maniacal idea.
—Germaine Greer

Polygamy is dumb fun. Monogamy requires much more sensitivity.
—Warren Beatty

The happiest time of anyone's life is just after the first divorce.
—John Kenneth Galbraith

Security is mostly superstition.
—Helen Keller

Did you hear about the fellow who blamed arithmetic for his divorce? His wife put two and two together.
—Earl Wilson

Love is a many-splintered thing.
—R. Buckminster Fuller

I hate to be a failure. I hate and regret the failure of my marriages. I would gladly give all my millions for just one lasting marital success.
—**J. Paul Getty**

To catch a husband is an art; to hold him is a job.
—**Simone de Beauvoir**

The best way to hold a man is in your arms.
—**Mae West**

Music is my mistress, and she plays second fiddle to no one.
—**Duke Ellington**

A miserable marriage can wobble along for years until something comes along and pushes one of the people over the brink. It's usually another man or woman. For me, it was a whole production staff and camera crew.
—**Pat Loud**

Love is supreme and unconditional; like is nice but limited.
—**Duke Ellington**

The story of a love is not important—what is important is that one is capable of love.
—**Helen Hayes**

She is an extremely beautiful woman, lavishly endowed by nature with but a few flaws in the masterpiece: she has an insipid double chin, her legs are too short, and she has a slight pot-belly. She has a wonderful bosom, though.
—**Richard Burton,** on Elizabeth Taylor

We all suffer from the preoccupation that there exists . . . in the loved one, perfection.
—**Sidney Poitier**

A false enchantment can all too easily last a lifetime.
—**W. H. Auden**

When you get married you forget about kissing other women.
—**Pat Boone**

God is a maker of marriages, but I wonder if He would bother to come to some of the affairs He has arranged?
—Harry Golden

"
I've only slept with the men I've been married to. How many women can make that claim?
—Elizabeth Taylor

WIDE WORLD PHOTOS
"

Sensual pleasures have the fleeting brilliance of a comet; a happy marriage has the tranquillity of a lovely sunset.
—Ann Landers

Love in marriage is commitment. Commitment involves a woman's full surrender to her man.
—Marabel Morgan

For some reason, it seems that the bride generally has to make more effort to achieve a successful marriage than the bridegroom.
—Elizabeth Post

As usual there's a great woman behind every idiot.
—**John Lennon**

Behind every successful man you'll find a woman who has nothing to wear.
—**James Stewart**

Throughout history, females have picked providers for males. Males pick anything.
—**Margaret Mead**

Men often marry their mothers. . . .
—**Edna Ferber**

A man usually marries because he wants to "cure" his mother.
—**Cary Grant**

A man's home may seem to be his castle on the outside; inside, it is more often his nursery.
—**Clare Boothe Luce**

We haven't ruled the possibility of children out. I figure I'm the blessed event in our family.
—**Dick Cavett**

The only time a woman really succeeds in changing a man is when he's a baby.
—**Natalie Wood**

Why does a woman work ten years to change a man's habits and then complain that he's not the man she married?
—**Barbra Streisand**

American women are good mothers, but they make poor wives.
—**Margaret Mead**

A wife, so often, is her mother.
—**Gail Sheehy**

Every bride has to learn it's not her wedding but her mother's.
—**Luci Johnson Nugent**

In our society it is an advantage to a young lady to be married rather than to live with somebody. So, if you love a young lady, why not give her all of the advantages?
—Jim Brown

A man in love is incomplete until he has married. Then he's finished.
—Zsa Zsa Gabor

There is only one terminal dignity—love.
—Helen Hayes

I will never make a statement that I would never ever remarry.
—Elizabeth Taylor

I knew her when she didn't know where her next husband was coming from.
—Anne Baxter

The art of love . . . is largely the art of persistence.
—Dr. Albert Ellis

Time in love and time in life are unrelated: forever exists more than once.
—Ned Rorem

Getting divorced just because you don't love a man is almost as silly as getting married just because you do.
—Zsa Zsa Gabor

Marriages are not eternal, so why should divorce be?
—Jean-Pierre Aumont

It seems the older men get, the younger their new wives get.
—Elizabeth Taylor

An archaeologist is the best husband any woman can have: the older she gets the more interested he is in her.
—Agatha Christie

Divorce is defeat. . . . It's an adult failure.
—Lucille Ball

For some reason, we see divorce as a signal of failure despite the fact that each of us has a right and an obligation to rectify any other mistake we make in life.
—Dr. Joyce Brothers

The worst thing that two people who've loved each other can do is to distort . . . the past. It is the single cruelest, and the one unforgivable, thing that one lover can do to another.
—Mike Nichols

Once a woman has forgiven her man, she must not reheat his sins for breakfast.
—Marlene Dietrich

The ultimate betrayal is not a wandering wife, but a wandering wife who tells her lover that her husband doesn't make as much as everyone thinks.
—Harry Golden

The best proof of love is trust.
—Dr. Joyce Brothers

She was the type that would wake up in the morning and *immediately* start apologizing.
—Woody Allen

No man is a hero to his wife's psychiatrist.
—Eric Berne

I'm officially resigning as the prime minister's wife.
—Margaret Trudeau

I had to give up Martha to become the attorney general's wife.
—Martha Mitchell

A man's job, basically, is to tame this world: a wife's job is to control herself—and indirectly her husband.
—Ruth Stafford Peale

Michael stands for hours for his operations and he'll stand for this.
—Mrs. Michael DeBakey, on her wedding day

A Mafia wife can hate her husband, but something she never does is divorce him while he is in jail.
—**Barbara Fuca**

Trouble is a part of your life, and if you don't share it, you don't give the person who loves you a chance to love you enough.
—**Dinah Shore**

Life is what happens to you when you're making other plans.
—**Betty Talmadge,** divorced wife of Senator Herman Talmadge

Our society is set up so that most women lose their identities when their husbands die. . . . It's wrenching enough to lose the man who is your lover, your companion, your best friend, the father of your children, without losing yourself as well.
—**Lynn Caine**

Memory is more indelible than ink.
—**Anita Loos**

The story of love is hello and good-by . . . until we meet again.
—**Jimi Hendrix**

11
Chic

JACQUELINE KENNEDY set the style in American fashion in 1960 when she became the first lady of the jet set. Her "thin look" redefined sensuality as a flat chest, pillbox hat, and Kenneth hair-do. In short hair and mini, Twiggy epitomized the leggy image—proving that even a boyish physique could be very sexy.

With the cultural revolution of the 1960s, fashion became self-expression. The dominant style was mod: a loose-fitting "do your own thing" look imported from the hippies on Carnaby Street in London. Men were now wearing flowered shirts. Women were marching into the office in boots, and, for the first time, both the sexes were wearing the pants.

In the 1970s, freak fashion softened into a healthy outdoor look typified by model Lauren Hutton. Cosmetic artist Way Bandy originated a natural beauty through make-up that brought out the "inner glow" of the American woman. Evening gowns disappeared from the scene. Jogging suits were in. The couturier departments of Saks, Bergdorf's, and Bendel's were now specialists in designer jeans!

Fashions fade, style is eternal.
—**Yves Saint Laurent**

The only thing ever constant in the fashion business is change.
—Halston

> 66
>
> Fashionable men and women don't just put on fashionable clothes. . . . The truly fashionable are beyond fashion.
> —Cecil Beaton
>
>
>
> UNITED PRESS INTERNATIONAL PHOTO
>
> 99

I base most of my fashion taste on what doesn't itch.
—Gilda Radner

I don't think the American woman has any vestige of originality or any special thing of her own. Nor does she want them. Let's face it, all she wants is to be popular.
—Diana Vreeland

She is sexy, witty, and dry-cleaned.
—Mary Quant's definition of the fashionable woman

Some of us are not great beauties. That notion is entirely responsible for whatever success I have had in life, because not being beautiful, I had to make up for it with brains, charm, drive, personality—you name it.
—Helen Gurley Brown

There are no ugly women, only lazy ones.
—Helena Rubenstein

The new bold beauty is round; she is not scrawny. She's sexy, earthy. She has fire and excitement in her eyes. Her body looks healthy, and strong enough so you could wrestle and roll with her.
—Francesco Scavullo

Zest is the secret of all beauty. There is no beauty that is attractive without zest.
—Christian Dior

Energy is beauty—a Ferrari with an empty tank doesn't run.
—Elsa Peretti

There will always be glamorous women who declare they do nothing special to maintain their trim, attractive bodies; a zest for living is what keeps you young, they proclaim. I do not envy them; I just don't believe a word they say.
—Luciana Avedon

Fashion is made by fashionable people.
—Halston

Fashion is finding something you're comfortable in and wearing it into the ground.
—Tuesday Weld

The jean. The jean is the destruction. It is the dictator. It is destroying creativity. The jean must be stopped.
—Pierre Cardin

Blue jeans? They should be worn by farm girls milking cows!
—Yves Saint Laurent

Saint Laurent has excellent taste. The more he copies me, the better taste he displays.
—**Coco Chanel**

There is no such thing as good or bad taste, except in the eyes of a snob.
—**John Fairchild,** publisher of *Women's Wear Daily*

What's in a name? A 35 percent markup.
—**Vince Thurston,** manager of T. Anthony leathergoods store

My clothes are addressed to women who can afford to travel with forty suitcases.
—**Yves Saint Laurent**

No woman is ever too slim or too rich.
—**Mrs. William (Babe) Paley**

I don't think chic has anything to do with money. You can have all the money in the world and have no idea what elegance means.
—**Bianca Jagger**

I love the "bag ladies" at Grand Central Station—they're the real Sonia Rykiels of the world, the original designers of the layered look.
—**Blair Sabol**

We should all just smell well and enjoy ourselves more.
—**Cary Grant**

Eat plenty of garlic. This guarantees you twelve hours of sleep—alone—every night, and there's nothing like rest to give you shining orbs.
—**Chris Chase**

What is elegance? Soap and water!
—**Cecil Beaton**

There is no such thing as an ugly woman—there are only the ones who do not know how to make themselves attractive.
—**Christian Dior**

I thank God for high cheekbones every time I look in the mirror.
—Suzy Parker

What does a woman need to know in order to design her face with cosmetics? Only her skin and her bones.
—Way Bandy

The most beautiful make-up of a woman is a passion. But cosmetics are easier to buy.
—Yves Saint Laurent

In the factory we make cosmetics; in the drugstore we sell hope.
—Charles Revson

Illusion is the secret of beauty.
—George Masters

Women who live for the next miracle cream do not realize that beauty comes from a secret happiness and equilibrium within themselves.
—Sophia Loren

Most of God's children are, in fact, barely presentable. The most common error made in matters of appearance is the belief that one should disdain the superficial and let the true beauty of one's soul shine through. If there are places on your body where this is a possibility, you are not attractive—you are leaking.
—Fran Lebowitz

I'm tired of all this nonsense about beauty being only skin-deep. That's deep enough. What do you want—an adorable pancreas?
—Jean Kerr

It's a good thing that beauty is skin deep, or I'd be rotten to the core.
—Phyllis Diller

There is beauty in everybody. You are born with it. It's just a matter of what you do with it, and if you lose it, it's like losing your soul.
—Francesco Scavullo

If truth is beauty, how come no one has their hair done in the library?
—**Lily Tomlin**

All you need in life is clean underwear and a good haircut.
—**Blair Sabol**

Hair is another name for sex.
—**Vidal Sassoon**

The second most important man in a woman's life has got to be her hairdresser.
—**Letitia Baldridge**

It's an ill wind that blows when you leave the hairdresser.
—**Phyllis Diller**

I don't know how long I like my egg boiled, but it's exactly right by the time I've finished my hair.
—**Betty Furness**

All happiness depends on a leisurely breakfast.
—**John Gunther**

Life itself is the proper binge.
—**Julia Child**

The only way you can stay as skinny as I am at my age is to starve.
—**Helen Gurley Brown**

Eating is self-punishment; punish the food instead. Strangle a loaf of Italian bread. Throw darts at a cheesecake. Chain a lamb chop to the bed. Beat up a cookie.
—**Gilda Radner**

Cheese—milk's leap toward immortality.
—**Clifton Fadiman**

"Roast Beef Medium" is not only a food. It is a philosophy.
—**Edna Ferber**

What is sauce for the goose may be sauce for the gander but it is not necessarily sauce for the chicken, the duck, the turkey, or the guinea hen.
—**Alice B. Toklas**

Thin people are beautiful but fat people are adorable.
—**Jackie Gleason**

Never in the history of fashion has so little material been raised so high to reveal so much that needs to be covered so badly.
—**Cecil Beaton,** on the mini-skirt

The midi was un-American, it was subversive, it was against the best instincts and the finest qualities of this great nation.
—**James Brady,** former publisher of *Women's Wear Daily*

What is important in a dress is the woman who's wearing it.
—**Yves Saint Laurent**

I dress for women—and I undress for men.
—**Angie Dickinson**

There are three intolerable things in life—cold coffee, lukewarm champagne, and overexcited women.
—**Orson Welles**

The perfect wife never complains about not having a thing to wear. She wears recycled patched denim, and when she and the perfect husband are dressing up to go out, *she's* ready first.
—**Lois Gould**

When in doubt, wear red.
—**Bill Blass**

When a woman dresses up for an occasion, the man should become the black velvet pillow for the jewel.
—**John Weitz,** Coty Award winner

Big girls need big diamonds.
—**Margaux Hemingway**

One can safely assume that a person who finds it necessary to consult a bracelet on the subject of his own state of mind is a person who is undoubtedly perplexed by a great many things.
—Fran Lebowitz

Style is self-plagiarism.
—Alfred Hitchcock

The only thing people are interested in is people.
—Diana Vreeland

A gossip is one who talks to you about others; a bore is one who talks to you about himself; and a brilliant conversationalist is one who talks to you about yourself.
—Lisa Kirk

To understand a society it is essential to understand how people climb. If there are more than two people together, if there are three, one of them is climbing.
—Sally Quinn

Deep breaths are very helpful at shallow parties.
—Barbara Walters

In Palm Beach you do not ever get divorced during the season.
—Charlotte Curtis

Nothing succeeds like address.
—Fran Lebowitz

I'm not really barred by anything except a certain kind of middle-class pretentiousness. I've always said I can go first-class or third. But I could never go second.
—Truman Capote

I never said "I want to be alone." I only said "I want to be let alone."
—Greta Garbo

He who does not enjoy his own company is usually right.
—Coco Chanel

Women are most fascinating between the ages of thirty-five and forty, after they have won a few races and know how to pace themselves. Since few women ever pass forty, maximum fascination can continue indefinitely.
—**Christian Dior**

You're never too old to become younger.
—**Mae West**

Pleasure is everything.
—**Diana Vreeland**

12
Media

WITH THE PHRASE "the medium is the message," Marshall McLuhan turned on the awareness of a turned-off generation to the power of communications. The Free Speech Movement at Berkeley had given birth to the New Journalism: a tell-it-like-it-is style translated into a vital siege of investigative reporting in such influential publications as the *New York Times*, the *Washington Post*, the *Los Angeles Free Press*, the *Berkeley Barb*, the *Village Voice* and *Rolling Stone*. The press quickly developed into the fourth branch of government.

Journalists like Norman Mailer, Jimmy Breslin, Tom Wolfe, and Gloria Steinem moved into the influential spotlight once dominated exclusively by politicians. Bob Woodward and Carl Bernstein became national heroes for breaking the scandal of Watergate. Daniel Ellsberg was all but lionized by the liberal establishment for the Pentagon Papers.

By the 1970s, the enrollment in journalism schools in the United States had nearly doubled. Ironically, in this new generation of journalists are descendants of the old generation of politicians. In the past five years, Caroline Kennedy, Julie and David Eisenhower, Linda Bird Johnson Robb, Jack and Susan Ford, not to mention Margaret Trudeau, have all debuted as writers or photographers for leading publications. At this time only Amy Carter is apparently sticking to politics—still unseduced by the power of the press.

"The Medium is the Message" because it is the medium that shapes and controls the search and form of human associations and action.
—**Marshall McLuhan**

I tape, therefore I am.
—**Studs Terkel**

A good newspaper is a nation talking to itself.
—**Arthur Miller**

News is the first rough draft of history.
—**Benjamin Bradlee,** editor of the *Washington Post*

Accuracy is to a newspaper what virtue is to a lady, but a newspaper can always print a retraction.
—**Adlai Stevenson**

A newspaper may somewhat arrogantly assert that it prints "all the news that's fit to print." But no newspaper yet has been moved to declare at the end of each edition, "That's the way it is," as Walter Cronkite does.
—**Eugene McCarthy**

Our major obligation is not to mistake slogans for solutions.
—**Edward R. Murrow**

Newspapers don't change tastes. They reflect taste.
—**Rupert Murdoch**

If a newspaper prints a sex crime, it's smut, but when the *New York Times* prints it, it's a sociological study.
—**Adolph S. Ochs**

A dilemma has to get up pretty early in the morning to fool the *New York Times.*
—**Edwin Newman**

The emergence of the press as a power in American life is directly proportionate to the failure of the other branches of our society to perform their historic assigned functions.
—**Norman Cousins**

As reporters, we should stay the hell out of politics and maintain a private position on any issue.
—**John Chancellor**

Journalists are now celebrities.
—**Nora Ephron**

This is the age of the journalist, more than the age of the artist, the teacher, the pastor. It is the age of "non-fiction" because imagination cannot keep up with the fantastic daily realities.
—**Eric Sevareid**

Some things can only be said in fiction, but that doesn't mean they are not true.
—**Aaron Latham**

A scoop is always most popular to the person who gets it.
—**David Frost**

Journalists are interesting. They just aren't as interesting as the things they cover.
—**Nora Ephron**

There are honest journalists like there are honest politicians. When bought, they stay bought.
—**Bill Moyers**

Journalists were never intended to be the cheerleaders of a society, the conductors of applause, the sycophants. Tragically, that is their assigned role in authoritarian societies, but not here—not yet.
—**Chet Huntley**

As you may know, I have many good friends in the press who, unfortunately, have thus far refused to identify themselves and go public.
—**Frank Sinatra**

The first essence of journalism is *to know what you want to know;* the second, is to find out who will tell you.
—**John Gunther**

A general journalist is jack-of-all-trades and master of none, save the trade of being jack-of-all.
—Eric Sevareid

Our job is only to hold up the mirror—to tell and show the public what has happened, and then it is the job of the people to decide whether they have faith in their leaders or government. We are faithful to our profession in telling the truth. That's the only faith to which journalists need adhere.
—Walter Cronkite

The journalist's job is to get the story by breaking into their offices, by bribing, by seducing people, by lying, by anything else to break through the palace guard.
—Robert Scheer

Journalism, like history, is certainly not an exact science.
—John Gunther

The best way to get thrown out of the columnists' club is to be uncertain about anything whatsoever on this earth.
—Eric Sevareid

Journalism is a kind of profession, or craft, or racket, for people who never wanted to grow up and go out into the real world. If you're a good journalist, what you do is live a lot of things vicariously, and report them for other people who want to live vicariously.
—Harry Reasoner

Guerrilla journalism came about because we didn't want to be part of access journalism. We hung out at parties and eavesdropped and stole memos and every other damn thing to crash through.
—Robert Scheer

The press is a little like the blackbirds in the fall—one flies off the telephone line, the others all fly away; and the other one comes back and sits down and they all circle and they all come down and sit . . . in a row again.
—Eugene McCarthy

Every nuance becomes a news story.
—George McGovern

The guys from the . . . Columbia Journalism School make the blunders. I'm from Ozone Park. Aqueduct Racetrack. There are no blunders allowed.
—Jimmy Breslin

My work is being destroyed almost as soon as it is printed. One day it is being read; the next day someone's wrapping fish in it.
—Al Capp

Is there any other industry in this country which seeks to presume so completely to give the customer what he does not want?
—Rupert Murdoch, publisher of the New York Post

The freedom of the press works in such a way that there is not much freedom from it.
—Princess Grace of Monaco

I can get a better grasp of what is going on in the world from one good Washington dinner party than from all the background information NBC piles on my desk.
—Barbara Walters

If you keep your mind sufficiently open, people will throw a lot of rubbish into it.
—William A. Orton

Freedom of the press is limited to those who own one.
—A. J. Liebling

Hitler said that he always knew you could buy the press. What he didn't know was you could get them cheap.
—Mort Sahl

A newspaper is the lowest thing there is.
—Mayor Richard Daley

Some newspapers are fit only to line the bottom of birdcages.
—**Spiro T. Agnew**

The real news is bad news.
—**Marshall McLuhan**

All advertising is good news.
—**Marshall McLuhan**

I won't buy a magazine that will publish what I write.
—**Goodman Ace**

If truth is less shapely than fiction, still it is more honest.
—**Geoffrey Wolff**

The truth about a man lies first and foremost in what he hides.
—**André Malraux**

Today it is the political novelist, not the political reporter, who conveys to us whatever truth there is to be gotten out of Washington.
—**Gay Talese**

The best mind-altering drug is truth.
—**Lily Tomlin**

The city room is an outhouse. You can get black lung just by working on the rewrite desk for a week. They should pass a law against the joint.
—**Jimmy Breslin**

One does not escape taxes or death or win arguments with the city desk.
—**Warren Hickle**

Instead of just recording reality, photographs have become the norm for the way things appear to us, thereby changing the very idea of reality and of realism.
—**Susan Sontag**

Hello from the gutters of New York City, which are filled with dog manure, vomit, stale wine, urine, and blood. But I am still here like a spirit roaming the night. Thirsty, hungry, seldom stopping to rest; anxious to please Sam.
—**Letter from David ("Son of Sam") Berkowitz,** to Jimmy Breslin, June 1, 1977

He's the only person I know who understands the proper use of the semicolon.
—**Jimmy Breslin,** on "Son of Sam," after receiving this letter

Writing a letter to a newspaper editor is the easiest way to gain prestige in America.
—**Harry Golden**

Oh, why do all you American journalists ask the same question? What factory do you come out of?
—**Yevgeny Yevtushenko,** to Barbara Walters

The questions are brutal because research of truth is a kind of surgery.
—**Oriana Fallaci**

In the realm of human destiny, the depth of man's questioning is more important than his answers.
—**André Malraux**

While the right to talk may be the beginning of freedom, the necessity of listening is what makes the right important.
—**Walter Lippmann**

There is no news, there's only media.
—**Susan Halas**

Reporters are puppets. They simply respond to the pull of the most powerful strings.
—**Lyndon Baines Johnson**

A reporter is as close to the action as a crablouse to the begetting of a child.
—**Norman Mailer**

A good reporter remains a skeptic all his life.
—**Jack Smith**

Half of the reporters in town are looking on you as a Pulitzer Prize waiting to be won.
—**Senator Lawton Chiles**

The challenge is to preserve the truth of that person without distorting what the person says.
—**Studs Terkel**

A writer needn't go out and live, but stay home and invent.
—**Ned Rorem**

A freelancer lives at the end of a sawed-off limb.
—**Catherine Breslin**

It is the rule, not the exception, that otherwise unemployable public figures inevitably take to writing for publication.
—**Richard Condon**

They have done better by me in the *Times* on my poetry than they have on my politics.
—**Eugene McCarthy**

Censorship, like charity, should begin at home; but, unlike charity, it should end there.
—**Clare Boothe Luce**

If the reader buys it, it's moral.
—**Steve Dunleavy,** reporter for the *New York Post*

If a senator is putting his hand on my fanny and telling me how he's going to vote on impeaching President Nixon, I'm not so sure I'm going to remove his hand no matter how demeaning it is.
—**Sally Quinn**

Maxine Cheshire makes you want to commit murder. Sally Quinn makes you want to commit suicide.
—**Henry Kissinger**

Men all over the country need *Hustler*. They feel inferior, and they are. Women are naturally superior; they're our only hope. I mean, my mother lives with me.
—**Larry Flynt**

Instead of hustling for sex, we'll be hustling for the Lord.
—**Larry Flynt,** after being "born again"

I don't have any fixed ideas on what's right and wrong. If I did, I would probably be writing editorials in newspapers.
—**James Earl Ray**

We've uncovered some embarrassing ancestors in the not-too-distant past. Some horse thieves, and some people killed on Saturday nights. One of my relatives, unfortunately, was even in the newspaper business.
—**Jimmy Carter,** on being presented a copy of his family tree

In October 1974, I started investigating the government's intelligence agencies; by February 1976, they were back investigating me.
—**Daniel Schorr**

All along, I was skeptical of this policy of deception, and yet I helped write some of those lies. I was well aware of them. I did not expose them.
—**Daniel Ellsberg,** on the Pentagon Papers, prior to fall 1969

The papers deal with high crimes by officials of our government. . . . These are issues of life and death, of war and peace. They're incomparably more important than what happens to me.
—**Daniel Ellsberg**

To stand out, for a man or a magazine, it is necessary to stand for something. Otherwise you stand still.
—**Arnold Gingrich**

Magazines all too frequently lead to books and should be regarded by the prudent as the heavy petting of literature.
—**Fran Lebowitz**

I felt as an American citizen, a responsible citizen, I could no longer cooperate in concealing this information from the American people. I took this action on my own initiative; and I am prepared for all the consequences.
—Daniel Ellsberg

The fact is that if the Pentagon Papers should have been made available before, as I think is widely accepted now, then there is damn little that should be kept secret.
—Daniel Ellsberg

Democracy depends on information circulating freely in society.
—Katherine Graham, publisher of the *Washington Post*

The ability of this country to keep secrets has gotten too good for our own good.
—Daniel Ellsberg

A government is the only known vessel that leaks from the top.
—James Reston

Intercourse between journalist and politician takes place by communiqué, by press conference, by interview, and by leak.
—Emery Kelen

The press conference is a politician's way of being informative without actually saying anything.
—Emery Kelen

The interview is an intimate conversation between journalist and politician wherein the journalist seeks to take advantage of the garrulity of the politician and the politician of the credulity of the journalist.
—Emery Kelen

Hubert Humphrey talks so fast that listening to him is like trying to read *Playboy* magazine with your wife turning the pages.
—Barry Goldwater

She doesn't need a steak knife. Rona cuts her food with her tongue.
—Johnny Carson, on Rona Barrett

I've got one tongue and it works pretty well.
—**Martha Mitchell**

I don't believe in that "no comment" business. I always have a comment.
—**Martha Mitchell**

I hate to look another human being in the eye and say, "No comment."
—**Andrew Young**

Rex Reed is either at your feet or at your throat.
—**Ava Gardner**

Gossip is the art of saying nothing in a way that leaves practically nothing unsaid.
—**Walter Winchell**

Gossip is when you hear something you like about someone you don't.
—**Earl Wilson**

Gossip is horrible. Gossip is suggestion without facts . . . and that we avoid.
—**Rupert Murdoch,** publisher of the *New York Post*

The constant fear of a performer is to become what is reflected back at you.
—**Linda Ronstadt**

Show me someone who never gossips, and I'll show you someone who isn't interested in people.
—**Barbara Walters**

A true celebrity was someone identifiable by name only.
—**Liz Smith**

The plain fact is that a celebrity is anyone *People* writes about.
—**Nora Ephron**

What we think we know is that young sells better than old, pretty sells better than ugly, sports figures don't do very well, TV sells better than music, music does better than movies, and anything does better than politics.
—**Richard Stolley,** managing editor, *People*

The mind boggles, baby.
—**Tom Wolfe**

News theater is any event that confuses news with theater and theater with news.
—**Robert Brustein**

Rock journalism is people who can't write interviewing people who can't talk for people who can't read.
—**Frank Zappa**

Mr. Paul Hume, music critic, *Washington Post,* Washington, D.C. Mr. Hume: I've read your review of my daughter Margaret's concert last night and I've come to the conclusion that you're an eight-ulcer man on four-ulcer pay. And after reading such poppycock, it's obvious that you're off the beam and that at least four of your ulcers are working overtime. I hope to meet you and when I do, you're going to need a new nose, plenty of beefsteak for black eyes, and perhaps a jockstrap below.
—**Harry S Truman,** upon reading a bad review of his daughter
   Margaret's singing

Now talk me out of it.
—**Benjamin Bradlee,** editor of the *Washington Post*

What, me worry?
—**Alfred E. Neuman**

I am constantly seduced by pure action.
—**Clay Felker**

Don't judge me by what you've heard about me, judge me by what I do.
—**Rupert Murdoch,** publisher of the *New York Post*

I always thought if you worked hard enough and tried hard enough, things would work out. I was wrong.
—**Katherine Graham,** publisher of the *Washington Post*

Change is the biggest story in the world today, and we are not covering it adequately.
—**James Reston,** in a 1963 address to Columbia University

And that's the way it is . . . and most of the time we hope it isn't.
—**Walter Cronkite**

13
"Chappaquiddick"

ON JULY 18, 1969, Senator Edward M. Kennedy drove his car off a bridge on Chappaquiddick Island and plunged into the deepest waters of his political career.

I do not seek to escape responsibility for my actions by placing the blame either on physical or emotional trauma brought on by the accident or anything else. I regard as indefensible the fact that I did not report the accident to the police immediately.
—**Edward M. Kennedy,** August 1, 1969

After all, even a politician is human.
—**Mike Mansfield,** Senate majority leader

I know what happened there and I'm the only one who knows. There's nothing else that can be said about it.
—**Edward M. Kennedy**

This thing has a long fuse. This is the fall of the House of Kennedy.
—**Former staff member** of President Johnson, August 4, 1969

14
Jocks

In 1961, Roger Maris broke Babe Ruth's long-standing record by hitting sixty-one home runs in the expanded 162-game season. Another of the Babe's records was broken on April 8, 1974, when Henry Aaron hit his 715th career home run against Al Downing of the Los Angeles Dodgers. Also in 1974, the fleet Lou Brock set a new all-time high by stealing 118 bases in a single season.

However, Catfish Hunter set a different kind of record for baseball in 1975 when he scored high against Yankee management by walking home—with a seven figure contract. Up until that time, the only other athlete to jump into this high tax bracket scored his points in basketball. After retiring from the court as the highest-paid player in history, Wilt ("The Stilt") Chamberlain added inches to his stature by signing a $1.8 million contract in 1973 to coach the San Diego Conquistadors. As the field became more crowded with free agents, players and their lawyers were warming up in the bullpen for the big play of the 1970s: the million-dollar contract for the All-American jock.

When you're as great as I am, it's hard to be humble.
—**Muhammad Ali**

Winning isn't everything. It's the only thing.
—**Vince Lombardi**

I always turn to the sports page first. The sports page records people's accomplishments; the front page has nothing but man's failures.
—**Earl Warren**

Fear of losing is what makes competitors so great. Show me a . . . gracious loser and I'll show you a perennial loser.
—**O. J. Simpson**

The taste of defeat has a richness of experience all its own.
—**Bill Bradley**

66

Love is more important than what we can take. . . . Please say with me, three times—Love! Love! Love!
—**Pélé,** in his speech upon officially retiring from professional soccer, 1977

UNITED PRESS INTERNATIONAL PHOTO

99

Everybody is saying that I might be the most unpopular champion in the history of Wimbledon. . . . But what do I care? Because I *am* the champion.
—**Jimmy Connors**

When we won the league championship, all the married guys on the club had to thank their wives for putting up with all the stress and strain all season. I had to thank all the single broads in New York.
—**Joe Namath**

Different strokes for different folks.
—**Emlen Tunnell,** first black man ever elected to the Football Hall of Fame

Going to bed with a woman never hurt a ballplayer. It's staying up all night looking for them that does you in.
—**Casey Stengel**

Nice guys. Finish last.
—**Leo Durocher**

Sports do not build character. They reveal it.
—**Heywood Hale Broun**

Anyone who will tear down sports will tear down America. Sports and religion have made America what it is today.
—**Woody Hayes**

A school without football is in danger of deteriorating into a medieval study hall.
—**Vince Lombardi**

Sport is a product of human culture. America seems to need football at this stage of our social development. When you get ninety million people watching a single game on television, it . . . shows you that people need something to identify with.
—**Joe Paterno**

I'm not a stunt man. I'm not a daredevil. . . . I'm an explorer.
—**Evel Knievel**

Boxing is a great sport and a dirty business.
—**Ken Norton**

When it's all finished and I write a book, if I do, the title will be "The Only Thing Square Was the Ring."
—**Bob Biron,** manager of Ken Norton

I am boxing. The big money and all the popularity of this sport is because of me.
—**Muhammad Ali**

As men get older, the toys get more expensive.
—**Marvin Davis,** Denver oilman, after purchasing the Oakland A's for a figure rumored to be more than $12 million

Sports is the toy department of human life.
—**Howard Cosell**

If Howard Cosell was a sport, it would be Roller Derby.
—**Jimmy Cannon**

In the next issue of *Cosmopolitan,* Howard Cosell will be the centerfold with his vital organ covered—his mouth.
—**Burt Reynolds**

You don't really see a muscle as a part of you. . . . You see it as a thing. . . . You look at it and it doesn't even seem to belong to you. . . . You form it. Just like a sculpture.
—**Arnold Schwarzenegger**

There is nothing as good as bodybuilding to get your body tuned up and totally in shape. It doesn't matter whether you want speed or brute strength, whether you want to run or develop endurance power. The only activity that can build the entire body evenly and uniformly is progressive weight-resistance training.
—**Arnold Schwarzenegger**

If you watch a game, it's fun. If you play it, it's recreation. If you work at it, it's golf.
—**Bob Hope**

It took me seventeen years to get three thousand hits in baseball. I did it in one afternoon on the golf course.
—Henry Aaron

In golf you're always breaking a barrier. When you bust it, you set yourself a little higher barrier, and try to break that one.
—Jack Nicklaus

Jack has become a legend in his spare time.
—Chi Chi Rodriguez, on Jack Nicklaus

I'm playing like Tarzan—and scoring like Jane.
—Chi Chi Rodriguez

If you drink, don't drive. Don't even putt.
—Dean Martin

Drinking is not a spectator sport.
—Jim Brosnan

Racing is a game of inches and tenths of seconds. It's not any one thing you do better than the other guy, it's just that you may have mastered each little thing a little better, so you go through the corner a tenth of a second quicker.
—Peter Revson

All I had to do is keep turning left.
—George Robson, 1946 winner of the Indianapolis 500

The most difficult transition I had to make from athletics to every-day life was from knowing what I was going to do to not knowing.
—Mark Spitz

Football is not an ad-lib game.
—Chuck Knox

Jogging is very beneficial. It's good for your legs and your feet. It's also very good for the ground. It makes it feel needed.
—Snoopy

Bridge is a sport of the mind.
—Omar Sharif

Baseball is beautiful . . . the supreme performing art. It combines
in perfect harmony the magnificent features of ballet, drama, art,
and ingenuity.
—**Commissioner Bowie Kuhn**

I don't care what people think about me. Let them think what they
want. I know I'm not a flake.
—**Mark ("The Bird") Fidrych**

I was born for soccer, just as Beethoven was born for music.
—**Pélé**

Basketball can serve as a kind of metaphor for ultimate cooperation.
It is a sport where success, as symbolized by the championship,
requires that the dictates of community prevail over selfish personal
impulses.
—**Bill Bradley**

Football is an attempt to sell a blown-out, smacked-out people,
fighting inflation, the exploitation of their work, of their earth, of
Vietnamese and American Indians, that our system is still socially,
economically, and politically viable. Pro football keeps telling them
you can't be second-rate, you have to be winners. No matter who
you victimize, no matter how hard you work or who you sacrifice,
it's all worth it to be Number One.
—**Dave Meggysey,** linebacker for the St. Louis Cardinals, upon
   quitting professional football in 1969

Some people try to find things in this game that don't exist. Football
is two things. It's blocking and tackling.
—**Vince Lombardi**

When everything else breaks down, I don't hesitate to roam out of
the pocket and do the boogaloo.
—**Fran Tarkenton**

The football season is like pain. You forget how terrible it is until it
seizes you again.
—**Sally Quinn**

Is it normal to wake up in the morning in a sweat because you can't
wait to beat another human's guts out?
—**Joe Kapp,** former Minnesota Vikings quarterback

There's an innate killer instinct in me.
—Jimmy Connors

Hurt is in your mind.
—Harry Lombardi, to his son Vince

WHAM! WHAM! WHAM! . . . WHAM! WHAM! WHAM! . . . WHAM! WHAM! WHAM! . . . POP! POP!
—Muhammad Ali

Sporting events are not a safety valve but create even more aggression.
—Richard Leakey

The only time sex has bothered me is when I do it during the competition.
—Bruce Jenner

❝

There are some girls who are turned on by my body and some others who are turned off. But for the majority I just use it as a conversation piece. Like someone walking a cheetah down Forty-Second Street would have a natural conversation piece.
—Arnold Schwarzenegger

WIDE WORLD PHOTOS

❞

We've got to get women's tennis off the women's pages and into the sports pages.
—**Billie Jean King**

Women can't play a lick. I'll prove that. I'll set women's tennis back twenty years.
—**Bobby Riggs,** before his match with Billie Jean King

We've come a long way. Forty years ago women were playing tennis in floppy hats and funny dresses. Now Bobby Riggs is doing it.
—**Billie Jean King**

Margaret [Court] opened the door. Now I'm gonna shut it.
—**Billie Jean King,** on signing for the King-Riggs match

Men playing women? I hope it never comes. Everyone knows that the Number One woman can't beat the Number Thirty man. That would be the battle of the sexes and everybody would become masculine.
—**Chris Evert**

No one would undergo a sex change for a reason as shallow as playing tennis.
—**Dr. Renee Richards**

I am not interested in medals or titles. I don't need them. I need the love of the public and I fight for it.
—**Olga Korbut**

How you play the game is for college boys. When you're playing for money, winning is the only thing that matters.
—**Leo Durocher**

He is scared to lose, he is scared to win, he is scared of everything. Nastase does not have a brain; he has a bird fluttering around in his head.
—**Ion Tiriac**

Losers have tons of variety. Champions take pride in just learning to hit the same old boring winners.
—**Vic Braden**

It's a lonesome walk to the sidelines, especially when thousands of people are cheering your replacement.
—**Fran Tarkenton**

No one knows what to say in the loser's room.
—**Muhammad Ali**

I give the same halftime speech over and over. It works best when my players are better than the other coach's players.
—**Chuck Mills,** Wake Forest football coach

Sometimes you win in the first year under a new coach on enthusiasm and vitality and newness alone. It's a kind of high unto itself. But, then, you have to find a way to keep it up when the romance is tailing off. That's the hard part. In football or any other marriage.
—**Tex Schramm,** general manager of the Dallas Cowboys

Last year wasn't all that bad. We led the league in flu shots.
—**Bill Fitch,** coach of the Cleveland Cavaliers

I'd rather be a football coach. That way you only lose eleven games a year.
—**Abe Lemons,** University of Texas basketball coach

Every time you win, you're reborn; when you lose, you die a little.
—**George Allen**

Becoming number one is easier than remaining number one.
—**Bill Bradley**

When you win, you're an old pro. When you lose, you're an old man.
—**Charley Conerly**

Hustle is another word for survival.
—**Whitey Reiner,** coach at Canarsie High School

Sweat plus scarifice equals success.
—**Charles O. Finley**

All coaches are thinking men, or else they wouldn't survive.
—**Joe Paterno**

If he wins, he can take the credit, but if he loses, he'll have to take the blame.
—**George Steinbrenner,** referring to former New York Yankees manager Billy Martin

The two of them deserve each other. One's a born liar, the other's convicted.
—**Billy Martin,** referring to Reggie Jackson and George Steinbrenner, before he tearfully resigned from the New York Yankees, July 23, 1978

I resent the charges that we intentionally blacked out the city to help save the Yankees. The blackout was an act of God, and even God couldn't save the Yankees.
—**Spokesman for Con Edison,** referring to the July 14, 1977 New York City blackout

Baseball is very big with my people. It figures. It's the only time we can get to shake a bat at a white man without starting a riot.
—**Dick Gregory**

The basketball is a tool that the black has now, same as maybe once he had a plow.
—**Willis Reed**

The worst prejudice in sports isn't skin color, it is size.
—**Calvin Murphy,** 5'9" guard for the Houston Rockets

The horse weighs one thousand pounds and I weigh ninety-five. I guess I'd better get him to cooperate.
—**Jockey Steve Cauthen**

A black man has to fight for respect in basketball, season after season. And I measure that respect in the figures on my contract.
—**Kareem Abdul-Jabbar**

Nobody in football is worth a million dollars! It's ridiculous!
—**Joe Paterno,** after turning down a $1.3 million offer to become
coach of the Boston Patriots

Everybody's negotiable.
—**Muhammad Ali**

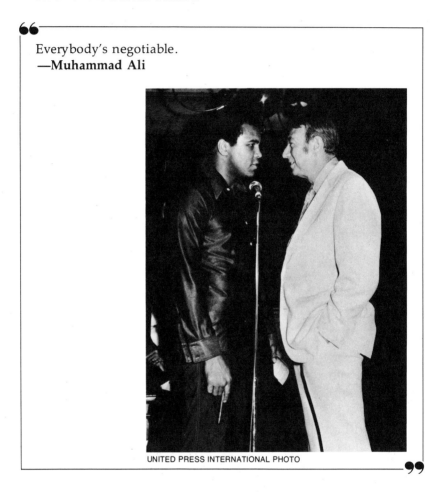

UNITED PRESS INTERNATIONAL PHOTO

I don't want to be liked, I just want to be respected.
—**Reggie Jackson**

I'm not an agent. I'm an engineer of careers.
—**Mark McCormach,** sports superagent

The real superstar is a man or a woman raising six kids on $150 a
week.
—**Spencer Haywood**

The question isn't at what age I want to retire, it's at what income.
—**George Foreman**

You're making too much at a young age. It isn't good for you.
—**M. Donald Grant,** chairman of the board of the New York
   Mets, to Tom Seaver, before Seaver was traded to the Cincin-
   nati Reds

A good professional athlete must have the love of a little boy. And
the good players feel the kind of love for the game that they did
when they were Little Leaguers.
—**Tom Seaver**

For the parent of a Little Leaguer, a baseball game is simply a nervous breakdown divided into innings.
—**Earl Wilson**

Trying to sneak a pitch past him is like trying to sneak the sunrise
past a rooster.
—**Amos Otis,** on Rod Carew

The way to catch a knuckleball is to wait until the ball stops rolling
and then pick it up.
—**Bob Uecker,** broadcaster

Ability: the art of getting credit for all the home runs somebody else
hits.
—**Casey Stengel**

Show me a starting pitcher who doesn't finish what he starts.
—**Sparky Lyle**

You don't save a pitcher for tomorrow. Tomorrow it may rain.
—**Leo Durocher**

If horses won't eat it, I don't want to play on it.
—**Dick Allen,** on Astroturf

Careful of what you write. The Mafia may come along and spray
garlic in your lawn.
—**Joe Garagiola,** warning sportswriters

All pro athletes are bilingual. They speak English and profanity.
—Gordie Howe

If you tell enough people in a press box your client played a great game, some will write it, whether he did nor not.
—Robert Woolf, sports attorney

The players and the reporters are bound together inextricably, like partners in a dance.
—Bill Bradley

All I have is natural ability.
—Mickey Mantle

I consider myself one of the best players baseball has had. I won't say the best, because there have been some great ones.
—Henry Aaron

I don't want to be Babe Ruth. He was a great ballplayer. I'm not try- ing to replace him. The record is there and damn right I want to break it, but that isn't replacing Babe Ruth.
—Roger Maris, during the 1961 season when he hit sixty-one home runs to set a new all-time baseball record

Statistics are about as interesting as first-base coaches.
—Jim Bouton

Why can't they understand the cold logic of it? I'm the straw that stirs the drink.
—Reggie Jackson

Look at this face, ain't a mark on it. No other fighter ever looked this way. I am The Greatest.
—Muhammad Ali

If you aren't fired with enthusiasm, you will be fired with enthusi- asm.
—Vince Lombardi

Winning isn't everything—but wanting to win is.
—Vince Lombardi

15
Nixon

ON JANUARY 20, 1969, persistence triumphed over a series of crushing political defeats when Richard Nixon was sworn in as the thirty-seventh president of the United States. He was re-elected in 1972 in a landslide—gaining 60.7 percent of the popular vote.

In his nearly six years as president, Nixon was heralded as a master of international diplomacy. With Secretary of State Henry Kissinger, he negotiated a cease-fire in the Middle East for the first time in twenty-five years, established a "dialogue" with Peking, and ended America's intense involvement in Vietnam. On August 8, 1974, Nixon insured himself perhaps an even more enduring place in American history by becoming the first president to resign under threat of impeachment.

Let us begin by committing ourselves to the truth—to see it like it is, and tell it like it is—to find the truth, to speak the truth, and to live the truth.

—**Richard Nixon,** accepting the presidential nomination in 1968

He not only doesn't give a damn about the people; he doesn't know how to tell the truth. I don't think the son of a bitch knows the difference between telling the truth and lying.
—**Harry S Truman,** on Richard Nixon

I made my mistakes, but in all my years of public life I have never profited, never profited from public service. I have earned every cent.
—**Richard Nixon**

The Nixon Political Principle: If two wrongs don't make a right—try three.
—**Laurence Peter**

I hear that whenever anyone in the White House tells a lie, Nixon gets a royalty.
—**Richard Nixon**

As I leave the press, all I can say is this: For sixteen years, ever since the Hiss case, you've had a lot of fun—a lot of fun—that you've had an opportunity to attack me. . . . Just think about how much you're going to be missing: you won't have Nixon to kick around any more, because, gentlemen, this is my last press conference.
—**Richard Nixon,** after losing the 1962 California gubernatorial election

I'm an introvert in an extrovert's profession.
—**Richard Nixon**

The essence of this man is loneliness.
—**Henry Kissinger,** on Richard Nixon

I'll have to have a room of my own. Nobody could sleep with Dick. He wakes up during the night, switches on the lights, speaks into his tape recorder.
—**Pat Nixon**

I'm not a lovable man.
—**Richard Nixon**

Call it paranoia, but paranoia for peace isn't that bad.
—**Richard Nixon**

You can't underestimate the power of fear.
—**Tricia Nixon Cox**

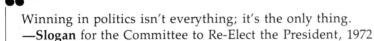

Winning in politics isn't everything; it's the only thing.
—**Slogan** for the Committee to Re-Elect the President, 1972

UNITED PRESS INTERNATIONAL PHOTO

I would walk over my grandmother if necessary to get Nixon re-elected!
—**Charles W. Colson**

Nixon can be beaten. He's like a Spanish horse who runs faster than anyone for the first nine lengths and then turns around and runs backward. He'll do something wrong in the end. He always does.
—**Lyndon Baines Johnson**

My strong point, if I have a strong point, is performance. I always produce more than I promise.
—**Richard Nixon**

We need this man of action, this man of accomplishment, this man of experience, this man of courage; we need this man of faith in America . . . who has brought us to the threshold of peace.
—**Nelson Rockefeller,** nominating Richard Nixon for his second presidential term, 1972

I never made the [football] team. . . . I was not heavy enough to play the line, not fast enough to play halfback, and not smart enough to be a quarterback.
—**Richard Nixon**

The election of 1972 simply goes to prove that America is a land where the lowest, most common man can become president. And he did.
—**Kirkpatrick Sale**

I like the job I have now, but, if I had my life to live over again, I'd like to have ended up as a sports writer.
—**Richard Nixon**

I have asked you for a moral and spiritual restoration in the land, and give thanks that in Thy sovereignty Thou hast permitted Richard M. Nixon to lead us at this momentous hour of our history.
—**The Reverend Billy Graham**

I would have made a good pope.
—**Richard Nixon**

Richard Nixon is a no-good lying bastard. He can lie out of both sides of his mouth at the same time, and if he ever caught himself telling the truth, he'd lie just to keep his hand in.
—**Harry S Truman**

It has often been said that Richard Nixon was a man without a home, a "rootless" figure, without a "stamp of place." . . . The fact is that Nixon bore very clearly the stamp of place, only the place was Southern California, and *that* was rootless and ill-defined, a mercurial, restless society.
—**Kirkpatrick Sale**

I won't go so far as to say he's insane. I will go so far as to say I find his behavior peculiar.
—**George McGovern,** on Richard Nixon

I believe President Nixon—like Abraham Lincoln—is a man uniquely suited to serve our nation in a time of crisis.
—**Gerald Ford**

I would rather be a one-term president . . . than a two-term president at the cost of seeing America become a second-rate power, and to see this nation accept the first defeat in its proved one-hundred-and-ninety-year history.
—**Richard Nixon,** 1970, on the announcement of the invasion of Cambodia

Nixon has a secret plan to end the war—he's voting for George McGovern.
—**Antiwar poster**

North Vietnam cannot defeat or humiliate the United States. Only Americans can do that.
—**Richard Nixon**

We were sitting in the bow of the yacht. I'm an old Navy man. The bow is the near end, isn't it?
—**Richard Nixon,** to David Frost in a televised interview

When you buy peace at any price it is always on the installment plan for another war.
—**Richard Nixon**

We live in an age of anarchy both abroad and at home.
—**Richard Nixon**

I should like to congratulate you on the nomination. However, I have reason to believe that the organization that has nominated you merely wishes you to hear of the nomination so that you can recover from the Watergate affair.
—**Idi Amin,** to President Nixon upon his 1972 nomination for the Nobel Peace Prize

Once you get into this great stream of history, you can't get out.
—**Richard Nixon**

To persevere in one's duty and remain silent is the best answer to calumny.
—**Tricia Nixon Cox,** quoting George Washington

A man is not finished when he's defeated; he's finished when he quits.
—**Richard Nixon**

16
──────────────────────────
Watergate

ON AUGUST 8, 1974, Richard Milhous Nixon secured his special niche in American history—as the first president of the United States to resign the nation's highest office under threat of impeachment. During the Watergate hearings, American politics had fallen to a new low, but through the integrity of such men and women as Judge John J. Sirica, Senator Sam Ervin, Representative Peter Rodino, Representative Barbara Jordan, and (then) Attorney General Elliot Richardson, the system proved stronger than its malefactors.

───────────────

We are all the president's men, and we've got to behave that way.
—**Henry Kissinger**

The first impression one gets of a ruler and of his brains is from seeing the men that he has about him.
—**Henry Kissinger,** quoting Machiavelli

I have an absolute rule. I refuse to make a decision that somebody else can make. The first rule of leadership is to save yourself for the

big decision. Don't allow your mind to become cluttered with the trivia. Don't let yourself become the issue.
—**Richard Nixon**

If you got 'em by the balls, their hearts and minds will follow.
—**Green Beret slogan,** above the bar in Charles Colson's den

When the going gets tough, the tough get going.
—**John Mitchell**

There was a cancer growing on the presidency, and if the cancer was not removed . . . the president himself would be killed by it.
—**John Dean**

I felt sure that it was just a public-relations problem that only needed a public-relations solution.
—**Richard Nixon**

We would joke about Colson's ever-expanding empire—the Department of Dirty Tricks, we called it—and about the fact that none of us knew exactly what Colson was up to. The joke in time would be on us.
—**Jeb Stuart Magruder**

I was not there to think; I was there to follow orders.
—**Bernard L. Barker,** Watergate burglar

If I've got a future, it's in government, and when the Big Man tells me to do something, either I do it for him or he gets someone else who can.
—**G. Gordon Liddy**

What really hurts in matters of this sort is not the fact that they occur, because overzealous people in campaigns do things that are wrong. What really hurts is if you try to cover up.
—**Richard Nixon**

I want you all to stonewall it; let them plead the Fifth Amendment, cover up or anything else, if it'll save it—save the plan.
—**Richard Nixon**

To support him they'll have to affirm the divine right of kings.
—**Sam Ervin,** referring to the Supreme Court decision on the
    Nixon tapes

I am totally unconcerned about anything other than getting the job
done. . . . Just so you understand me, let me point out that the
statement . . . "I would walk over my grandmother if necessary,"
is absolutely accurate.
—**Charles Colson**

This is a can of worms. . . . But the way you have handled all this
. . . has been very skillful, putting your fingers in the leaks that
have sprung here and sprung there.
—**Richard Nixon,** to John Dean

I don't give a damn how it is done; do whatever has to be done to
stop these leaks and prevent further unauthorized disclosures. . . .
I don't want excuses. I want results . . . whatever the cost.
—**Richard Nixon,** June 1971

He told us he was going to take crime out of the streets. He did. He
took it to the damn White House.
—**Reverend Ralph D. Abernathy**

When the president does it, that means it is not illegal.
—**Richard Nixon**

I am not a crook.
—**Richard Nixon**

I had expected to find all sorts of wrongdoing by his aides, conduct
unbecoming and even criminal, but it had never occurred to me
that the president was in the driver's seat.
—**Leon Jaworski**

My friends, let me make one thing clear. This is a nation of laws
and, as Abraham Lincoln said, no one is above the law, no one is
below the law. And we're going to enforce the law.
—**Richard Nixon,** 1968

The President *is* the government.
—**John Ehrlichman**

Law is the indispensable attribute of an ordered society.
—**Elliot Richardson**

You must pursue this investigation of Watergate even if it leads to the president. I'm innocent. You've got to believe I'm innocent. If you don't, take my job.
—**Richard Nixon,** to Elliot Richardson

I . . . have been guided by a simple principle, the principle that the law must deal fairly with every man. For me, this is the oldest principle of democracy. It is this simple but great principle which enables man to live justly and in decency in a free society.
—**Peter Rodino,** August 5, 1974

I can take it. . . . The tougher it gets, the cooler I get. . . .
—**Richard Nixon**

There are a lot of people who understand private morality who have no understanding of public morality.
—**William D. Ruckelshaus**

Rape is inevitable.
—**H. R. Haldeman,** April 14, 1973

Nothing less than the truth would sell.
—**John Dean**

I lost my ethical compass.
—**Jeb Stuart Magruder**

Once the toothpaste is out of the tube, it's hard to get it back in!
—**H. R. Haldeman**

It would have been simpler to have shot them all.
—**John Mitchell**

I have never analyzed what a Cabinet wife is, so I have continued to be Martha and I shall continue to be Martha.
—**Martha Mitchell**

John's problem was not Watergate. It was Martha.
—**Richard Nixon**

WIDE WORLD PHOTOS

Can you believe that a man can walk into your bedroom, take over, and pull the phone out of the wall? . . . They threw me down on the bed . . . and stuck a needle in my behind.
—**Martha Mitchell**

Why are the accusers doing this cruel thing to my father and the country? Is jealousy the name of this dangerous game? My father has accomplished what they could not accomplish.
—**Tricia Nixon Cox**

I deal in hardnose politics; you deal in crap.
—**Senator Lowell Weicker,** of Connecticut, to Charles Colson

Why is it there are so many more horses' asses than there are horses?
—**G. Gordon Liddy**

How could President Nixon have known so much about college football in 1969, and so little about Watergate in 1972?
—Joe Paterno

Every president needs an S.O.B.—and I'm Nixon's.
—H. R. Haldeman

Richard Nixon doesn't need a Cardinal Richelieu to advise him about anything.
—John Mitchell

When the prince approaches his lieutenant, the proper response of the lieutenant to the prince is *"Fiat voluntas tua"* (Thy will be done).
. . . I think I delayed things substantially. The prince was prince for a longer period of time.
—G. Gordon Liddy

O, what a tangled web we weave, when first we practice to deceive.
—Sam Ervin, during the Watergate hearings

If it hadn't been for Martha, there'd have been no Watergate, because John wasn't minding that store. . . . He was letting Magruder and all these boys, these kids, these nuts run this thing. He could only think of that poor Martha. . . .
—Richard Nixon

Somebody should get down and bleed for me. I try so hard.
—Martha Mitchell

It could have been a hell of a lot worse. They could have sentenced me to spend the rest of my life with Martha Mitchell.
—John Mitchell

Just because I don't know about politics the wolves have trampled me.
—Martha Mitchell

You really have to experience the feeling of being with the president in the oval office. . . . It's a disease I came to call Ovalitis.
—John Dean

The President seems to extend executive privilege way out past the atmosphere. What he says is executive privilege is nothing but executive poppycock.
—**Sam Ervin**

As President Nixon says, presidents can do almost anything, and President Nixon has done many things that nobody would have thought of doing.
—**Golda Meir**

I can see clearly now . . . that I was wrong in not acting more decisively and more forthrightly in dealing with Watergate. . . .
—**Richard Nixon**

You know I've always wondered about that taping equipment, but I'm damn glad we have it.
—**Richard Nixon,** to H. R. Haldeman

I personally listened to a number of them. The tapes are entirely consistent with what I know to be the truth and what I have stated to be the truth.
—**Richard Nixon,** on the White House tapes, July 24, 1974

There must be real dirt on the tapes; otherwise the president wouldn't be fighting so hard.
—**Henry Kissinger**

I would not like to be a Russian leader. They never know when they're being taped.
—**Richard Nixon**

No one is entitled to the truth.
—**E. Howard Hunt**

It's been my feeling that we're not as innocent as we said, or as guilty as they said.
—**David Eisenhower,** August 2, 1974

I gave 'em a sword. And they stuck it in, and they twisted it with relish. And I guess if I had been in their position, I'd have done the same thing.
—**Richard Nixon,** to David Frost in a televised interview, May 1977

It was basic police reporting. We talked to neighbors, friends, any-body. . . . But the work we did eventually paid off.
—**Bob Woodward**

These guys are damned able reporters. I have a high respect for them. But the tapestry they've woven is a bad one.
—**Richard Nixon,** on Woodward and Bernstein

Stay in there and battle.
—**Julie Nixon Eisenhower,** to her father

I've analyzed the best I can . . . and I have not found an impeach-able offense, and therefore resignation is not an acceptable course.
—**Richard Nixon,** August 6, 1974

Mistakes, yes. But for personal gain, never. You did what you be-lieved in. Sometimes right, sometimes wrong. And I only wish that I were a wealthy man—at the present time I have got to find a way to pay my taxes.
—**Richard Nixon**

There was no blackmail in Watergate. I define blackmail as getting something that is not your due. We regarded the funds as our due.
—**E. Howard Hunt**

All I want is a prosecution, not a persecution.
—**Richard Nixon,** on the firing of special prosecutor Archibald Cox

Whether ours shall continue to be a government of laws and not of men is now for Congress and ultimately the American people to decide.
—**Archibald Cox,** after being fired as special prosecutor

Watergate will be brought to an end by the constitutional process.
—**Richard Nixon,** August 6, 1974

We are all in it together. This is a war. We take a few shots and it will be over. We will give them a few shots and it will be over.
—**Richard Nixon,** September 15, 1972

We are a people in search of a national community. . . . It is a search that is unending, for we are not only trying to solve the problems of the moment. . . . But on a larger scale, we are attempting to fulfill the promise of America. . . .
—**Barbara Jordan**

America is not a place in geography; it's an idea. Watergate fouled up the idea.
—**Ted Van Dyk,** Nixon's chief speechwriter

This is, I say, the time for all good men not to go to the aid of their party, but to come to the aid of their country.
—**Eugene McCarthy**

Only the spirit that is not too sure it is right speaks for the values of civility and reason.
—**Archibald Cox,** June 25, 1974

Do people know what's going on in this country?
—**Ron Ziegler,** White House press secretary under Nixon

Those who take the long view of man's experience will find that from time to time there were other societies no less honest and courageous than ours in facing all the ugliness, cruelty, and indifference the mirror reveals, but with the greater honesty still to hold the brighter, nobler view of man and with the greater courage to pursue the vision.
—**Archibald Cox**

I have not lost faith in the nation's press.
—**Ron Ziegler,** February 14, 1974

The press . . . generally accepted and approved the methods of the *Washington Post* in its investigation of the Watergate case, even though the methods of the president's men and those of the *Post*'s men differed only slightly.
—**Eugene McCarthy**

If there is a Deep Throat, he's worth ten million dollars on the hoof.
—**Richard Reeves**

I think most people realize that I am politically naïve, and what I am saying represents my own viewpoint. . . . When I talk to anyone, I talk from the heart instead of the head.
—**Martha Mitchell**

I've always been able to sympathize with what Jonah . . . is reputed to have said after three days: "If you'd kept your mouth shut, this thing wouldn't have happened."
—**Sam Ervin**

If they want to put me in jail, let them. The best writing done by politicians has been done from jail.
—**Richard Nixon,** August 8, 1974

I suppose we should all sing "Bail to the Chief."
—**Senator Howard Baker**

While technically I did not commit a crime, an impeachable offense . . . these are legalisms, as far as the handling of this matter is concerned; it was so botched up, I made so many bad judgments. The worst one, mistakes of the heart, rather than the head. . . . But let me say, a man in that . . . top job—he's got to have a heart, but his head must always rule his heart.
—**Richard Nixon**

I don't look forward to wearing the scarlet letter of Watergate the rest of my life.
—**John Dean**

I went and lied; and I'm paying the price for that lack of will power.
—**John Ehrlichman**

I changed my registration from Republican to Democrat before I went to prison because I couldn't stand the idea of a Republican going to jail.
—**Charles Colson**

The trouble with Republicans is that when they get into trouble, they start acting like cannibals.
—**Richard Nixon**

If my husband knew anything about the Watergate break-ins, Mr. Nixon also knew about it. I think Nixon should say good-by, to give credibility to the Republican Party and to the United States. . . . He let the country down. Mr. President should retire.
—**Martha Mitchell**

Daddy's not a quitter.
—**Julie Nixon Eisenhower,** August 3, 1974

The president has always been a firm believer in the rule of the law.
—**James D. St. Clair,** chief White House defense counsel

When you're a lawyer, you expect your client to lie to you, but not when he is the president.
—**Dick Hauser,** assistant to the special White House counsel for Watergate

Never underestimate the power of a president.
—**Barbara Walters**

Why is it over?
—**David Eisenhower,** to Richard Nixon, August 2, 1974, after Nixon announced privately that he would resign

I would like to discuss the most important issue confronting this nation, and confronting us internationally too—inflation.
—**Richard Nixon,** to his cabinet two days before his resignation, August 6, 1974

The president was up walking the halls last night, talking to pictures of former presidents—giving speeches and talking to the pictures on the wall.
—**Edward Cox,** August 6, 1974

Henry, please don't ever tell anyone that I cried and that I was not strong.
—**Richard Nixon,** August 7, 1974

There'll be no tears. I haven't cried since Eisenhower died.
—**Richard Nixon,** August 7, 1974.

I hereby resign this office of president of the United States.
—**Richard Nixon,** August 8, 1974

By taking this action, I hope that I will have hastened the start of healing.
—**Richard Nixon,** August 8, 1974

Those who hate you don't win unless you hate them—and then you destroy yourself.
—**Richard Nixon,** in a farewell speech to the White House staff, August 9, 1974

I let the American people down, and I have to carry that burden with me for the rest of my life. My political life is over. I will never yet, and never again have an opportunity to serve in any official position. Maybe I can give a little advice from time to time.
—**Richard Nixon**

I saw both greatness and meanness in Nixon in such bewildering combination that, years later, peering out of a hotel window at the White House which I had been forced to leave, I muttered out loud: "Nixon was the weirdest man ever to live in the White House."
—**H. R. Haldeman**

I have impeached myself by resigning.
—**Richard Nixon**

The genius of impeachment lay in the fact that it could punish the man without punishing the office.
—**Arthur M. Schlesinger, Jr.**

Richard Nixon self-impeached himself. He gave us Gerald Ford as his revenge.
—**Bella Abzug**

There are lines at Lompoc prison that Bob cannot step across until he is released, but the walls at San Clemente are inescapable. There are all kinds of prisons. I'll take Lompoc.
—**Joanne Haldeman**

From Watergate we learned what generations before us have known; our Constitution works. And during Watergate years it was interpreted again so as to reaffirm that no one—absolutely no one—is above the law.
—**Leon Jaworski**

Watergate showed more strengths in our system than weaknesses. . . . The whole country did take part in quite a genuine sense in passing judgment on Richard Nixon.
—**Archibald Cox**

Our long national nightmare is over.
—**Gerald Ford,** in his inaugural address, August 9, 1974

17
"Generation Gap"

PAUL GOODMAN and Erik Erikson heralded the "generation gap" as a cause of the brewing social revolution. But in 1963 it was Bob Dylan who trumpeted the action in his song "Masters of War," which summoned American parents to recognize that their sons and daughters were now beyond their command.

The youth cult grew with the student riots at Berkeley in 1964, finally graduating into a national counterculture. The commencement ceremonies were staged as a demonstration in People's Park with Mario Savio, Jerry Rubin, and Abbie Hoffman giving the keynote addresses in four-letter rhetoric.

In uniforms of blue jeans, love beads, long hair, T-shirts, headbands, and sandals, the younger generation renounced their degrees (and parents' pedigrees) to "drop out of society and form a commune in the country." By 1968, however, youth was edging middle age out of power. Corporations, a last stronghold of maturity and responsibility, were now recruiting vice presidents whose major qualifications were a B.A. degree and an age under thirty.

Don't trust anyone over thirty!
—**Mario Savio**

There's nothing sadder than an old hipster.
—**Lenny Bruce**

We will not bury you: we will just outlive you.
—**Tom Hayden**

It is the missed revolutions of modern times—the fallings-short and the compromises—that add up to the conditions that make it hard for the young to grow up in our society.
—**Paul Goodman**

The generation gap is just another way of saying that the younger generation makes overt what is covert in the older generation; the child expresses openly what the parent represses.
—**Erik Erikson**

Even the Bible said that the young would be weaker but wiser.
—**Little Richard**

When you turn thirty, a whole new thing happens: you see yourself acting like your parents.
—**Blair Sabol**

Who would have guessed that maturity is only a short break in adolescence?
—**Jules Feiffer**

The ideal of American parenthood is to be a kid with your kid.
—**Shana Alexander**

Youth is not chronological age but the state of growing, learning, and changing. . . . All people must be helped to regain the condition of youth.
—**Charles Reich**

Youth has become a class.
—**Roger Vadim**

Adolescence is that period in a kid's life when his or her parents become more difficult.
—**Ryan O'Neal**

The plot against the family is a paper tiger.
—**Ellen Willis**

I am convinced that every boy, in his heart, would rather steal second base than an automobile.
—**Justice Tom C. Clark,** of the Supreme Court, on juvenile delinquency

The family that is busted together is adjusted together.
—**Timothy Leary**

Childhood is where "competition" is a baseball game and "responsibility" is a paper route.
—**Erma Bombeck**

The thing that impresses me most about America is the way parents obey their children.
—**The Duke of Windsor**

Parents are the bones on which children cut their teeth.
—**Peter Ustinov**

Kids are wonderful, but I like mine barbecued.
—**Bob Hope**

The hardest part of raising children is teaching them to ride bicycles. . . . A shaky child on a bicycle for the first time needs both support and freedom. The realization that this is what the child will always need can hit hard.
—**Sloan Wilson**

The easiest way to convince my kids that they don't really need something is to get it for them.
—**Joan Collins**

There is no such thing as personal responsibility. It's a contradiction in terms. Responsibility for children ends at birth.
—**Timothy Leary**

The family is the American fascism.
—**Paul Goodman**

There's no such thing as a kid who needs fixing. . . . They're born with everything. And what most people do is squash it and take it away from them.
—**Robert Blake**

When I was kidnapped my parents snapped into action; they rented out my room.
—**Woody Allen**

Teenage children are totally intolerant of midlife parents for having much the same romantic fantasies they have.
—**Gail Sheehy**

I've got nothin', Ma, to live up to.
—**Bob Dylan**

You say, "Here is the opportunity," and the youth of America says, "How much are you going to pay me?"
—**Casey Stengel**

They take their tactics from Castro and their money from Daddy.
—**Spiro T. Agnew**

Interest your kids in bowling. Get them off the streets and into the alleys.
—**Don Rickles**

The trouble with teenagers is that if you ask them the number that comes after nine, they tell you it's Operator.
—**Jackie Mason**

What's done to children, they will do to society.
—**Karl Menninger**

We can only know as adults what we can only feel as children.
—**Leslie Fiedler**

My mother loved children—she would have given anything if I had been one.
—**Groucho Marx**

The whole idea that children should be seen and not heard is archaic. Young people are not extensions of our egos, they are individuals unto themselves.
—**Henry Winkler**

A hippie wears his hair long like Tarzan, walks like Jane, and smells like Cheetah.
—**Buster Crabbe**

If a guy wants to wear his hair down to his ass, I'm not revolted by it. But I don't look at him and say, "Now there's a fella I'd like to spend next winter with."
—**John Wayne**

The older they get the better they were when they were younger.
—**Jim Bouton**

What's your road, man?—holyboy road, madman road, rainbow road, guppy road, any road. It's an anywhere road for anybody anyhow.
—**Jack Kerouac**

It seems to me a mistake to generalize people. They've been generalized so much—"the middle class," "the kids"—that a very odd thing has happened: they actually think of themselves as instances of a generality.
—**Mike Nichols**

When people tell you how young you look, they are also telling you how old you are.
—**Cary Grant**

When a man begins to *act* logically according to others . . . then he has left his youth behind.
—**Hortense Calisher**

Youth is a quality, not a matter of circumstances.
—**Frank Lloyd Wright**

Youth measures in only one direction . . . from things as they are to an ideal of what things ought to be, while the old measure things as they are against the past the old remember.
—**Archibald Cox**

Young people are moving away from feeling guilty about sleeping with somebody to feeling guilty if they are *not* sleeping with someone.
—**Margaret Mead**

While mother is busy in the kitchen studying a new recipe, the children are busy in the playroom studying each other.
—**Dr. David M. Reuben**

The young can seldom be faithless for long to the same person.
—**Mignon McLaughlin**

We youths say "like" all the time because we mistrust reality. It takes a certain commitment to say something is. Inserting "like" gives you a bit more running room.
—**James Kunen**

If the very old will remember, the very young will listen.
—**Chief Dan George**

People should be free to find or make for themselves the kinds of educational experiences they want their children to have.
—**John Holt**

Your children need your presence more than your presents.
—**Reverend Jesse Jackson**

It is easy enough to praise men for the courage of their convictions. I wish I could teach the sad young of this mealy generation the courage of their confusions.
—**John Ciardi**

Let the learner direct his own learning.
—**John Holt**

We all learn by experience but some of us have to go to summer school.
—**Peter De Vries**

The task of the modern educator is not to cut down jungles but to irrigate deserts.
—**C. S. Lewis**

I had nothing to offer anybody except my own confusion.
—**Jack Kerouac**

I saw the best minds of my generation destroyed by madness.
—**Allen Ginsberg**

Sometimes it's necessary to go a long distance out of the way in order to come back a short distance correctly.
—**Edward Albee**

The past went that-a-way.
—**Marshall McLuhan**

Old people don't get tired—it's only the young who tire. Confusion exhausts them.
—**George Balanchine**

There's no road back to childhood, but what fool would care to go?
—**Nicholas ("Nick The Greek") Dandolos**

The good still die young. Eternal youth—that's what you need. Nothing improves with age.
—**Lauren Bacall**

The hardest job kids face today is learning good manners without seeing any.
—**Fred Astaire**

If you don't run your own life, somebody else will.
—**John Atkinson,** educator

The correct way to raise a kid in America would be half by authority and half by explanation.
—**Herman Kahn**

Authority is not power; that's coercion. Authority is not knowledge; that's persuasion, or seduction. Authority is simply that the author has the right to make a statement and to be heard.
—**Herman Kahn**

When you are sixty-five, you have proven yourself already or you have not. It does not matter any more. We are no longer on the make.
—**S. I. Hayakawa,** elected to the California senate at age seventy-one

Time wounds all heels.
—**Ann Landers**

Old age is like a plane flying through a storm. Once you're aboard, there's nothing you can do.
—**Golda Meir**

Middle age is when your age starts to show around your middle.
—**Bob Hope**

Age changes our relationship with time: as the years go by our future shortens, while our pasts grow heavier.
—**Simone de Beauvoir**

Old age is like everything else. To make a success of it, you've got to start young.
—**Fred Astaire**

The three ages of man: youth, middle age, and "You're looking wonderful!"
—**Francis Cardinal Spellman**

Avoid the temptation to put too much stock in that well-worn adage about how it's all right to be a radical in your youth if you're conservative in your old age. The people who pronounce that one, it turns out, are old conservatives. The old radicals have a different way of looking at it.
—**Kirkpatrick Sale**

It is the malady of our age that the young are so busy teaching us that they have no time left to learn.
—**Eric Hoffer**

A university is what a college becomes when the faculty loses interest in students.
—**John Ciardi**

Colleges are like old-age homes; except for the fact that more people die in colleges.
—**Bob Dylan**

When a subject becomes totally obsolete we make it a required course.
—**Peter Drucker**

In university they don't tell you that the greater part of the law is learning to tolerate fools.
—**Doris Lessing**

We are people of this generation, bred in at least modest comfort, housed now in universities, looking uncomfortably to the world we inherit.
—**Tom Hayden**

By its dominant voices, its most unforgettable faces, and its chief acts of bravery does a generation recognize itself and history mark it.
—**Eric Sevareid**

Confusion is mightier than the sword.
—**Abbie Hoffman**

Do not weep for them, America. Your children, far braver than you, were a moment in the conscience of man.
—**Mark Lane**

It is better to err on the side of daring than the side of caution.
—**Alvin Toffler**

My poor brother started to drink when he was only fourteen. By the time he was twenty-one, he'd completely gone to pot.
—**Line** from Laugh-in

Who fits in any more? I was invited to a pot party and I brought Tupperware.
—**Joan Rivers**

Speed will turn you into your parents.
—**Frank Zappa**

It took twenty of us working twenty hours a day, six days a week for an entire year, to accomplish what one Dartmouth student now can do in one afternoon.
—**John Kemeny,** Dartmouth College president and an architect of the A-bomb, on the $15 calculator

Today's "fact" becomes tomorrow's "misinformation."
—**Alvin Toffler**

Fact and fancy look alike across the years that link the past with the present.
—**Helen Keller**

There is no yesterday, so what's left is today.
—**Bob Dylan**

Today's conformity is . . . the retreat from controversiality.
—**Herman Kahn**

The sixties was love, the seventies is cement.
—**Peter Beard**

Why must we have something to look forward to? Why can't we just look at now?
—**Jerry Rubin**

Where the Third Great Awakening will lead, who can presume to say? One only knows that the great religious waves have a momentum all their own. . . . And this one has the mightiest, holiest roll of all, the beat that goes . . . Me . . . Me . . . Me . . . Me. . . .
—**Tom Wolfe**

Life is a banquet and most poor sons-of-bitches are starving to death.
—**Auntie Mame**

Of all the "isms" that have plagued this century, ageism is the most stupid. It's time to declare war on the mindless Youth Cult that has our time in its grip, demoralizing our people, weakening our system . . . wasting our experience, betraying our democracy, and blowing out our brains.
—**Garson Kanin**

The entire movement to acquire antiques was born out of sheer respect for things that lasted longer than fifteen minutes.
—**Erma Bombeck**

The saddest aspect of old age is not . . . the imminence of death, but the realization that we have outlived our contemporaries.
—**Harry Golden**

The really frightening thing about middle age is the knowledge that you'll outgrow it.
—**Doris Day**

Old age isn't so bad when you consider the alternative.
—**Maurice Chevalier**

Death is, after all, the only universal experience except birth.
—**Stewart Alsop**

I'll never make the mistake of bein' seventy again!
—**Casey Stengel**

It has been said that there is no fool like an old fool—except a young fool. But the young fool has first to grow up to be an old fool to realize what a damn fool he was when he was a young fool.
—**Harold Macmillan**

By the time you're eighty years old you've learned everything. You only have to remember it.
—**George Burns**

You're never too old to become younger.
—**Mae West**

The one thing wrong with the younger generation is that I don't belong to it anymore.
—**Buddy Ebsen**

The only thing worthwhile when you grow older is watching people grow.
—**Frances Steloff**

Tomorrow is the most important thing in life. Comes into us at midnight very clean. It's perfect when it arrives and it puts itself in our hands. It hopes we've learned something from yesterday.
—John Wayne

I must be getting absent-minded. Whenever I complain that things aren't what they used to be, I always forget to include myself.
—George Burns

Middle age is when anything new in the way you feel is most likely a symptom.
—Laurence Peter

Middle age is when your clothes no longer fit, and it's you who need the alterations.
—Earl Wilson

As long as you are curious, you defeat age.
—Burt Lancaster

You know you're getting old when the candles cost more than the cake.
—Bob Hope

Life is like an onion: you peel it off one layer at a time, and sometimes you weep.
—Carl Sandburg

What youth is afraid of is that in old age the strength for protest will be gone, but the terror of life will remain.
—Harry Reasoner

Experience is what enables you to recognize a mistake when you make it again.
—Earl Wilson

Being seventy is not a sin.
—Golda Meir

18
Nostalgia

THE ROMANTICISM of the 1960s was rich in nostalgia: the matinee idols of the past had become the icons of "camp."

Never give a sucker an even break.
—**W. C. Fields**

Hello, suckers.
—**Humphrey Bogart,** in *Racket Busters*

The whole world is about three drinks behind.
—**Humphrey Bogart**

When I sell liquor, it's called bootlegging; when my patrons serve it on silver trays on Lake Shore Drive, it's called hospitality.
—**Al Capone**

Whatever you do, kid, always serve it with a little dressing.
—**George M. Cohan,** to Spencer Tracy

Play it, Sam.
—**Humphrey Bogart,** as Rick in *Casablanca*

Drown in a cold vat of whiskey? Death, where is thy sting?
—**W. C. Fields**

I didn't want to be born. You didn't want me to be born. It's been a calamity on both sides.
—**Bette Davis,** to her mother in *Now, Voyager*

I am forever flawed.
—**W. C. Fields**

Hearts will never be practical until they can be made unbreakable.
—**The Wizard of Oz,** to the Tin Man

Never try to impress a woman, because if you do she'll expect you to keep up to the standard for the rest of your life.
—**W. C. Fields**

I'm a very good man. I'm just a very bad wizard.
—**The Wizard of Oz**

I do not care to belong to a club that accepts people like me as members.
—**Groucho Marx,** on resigning from the Friars Club

Anybody who hates children and dogs can't be all bad.
—**W. C. Fields**

I'm probably a cad. Are you by any chance a weak woman?
—**Humphrey Bogart,** in *Men Are Such Fools*

It's late, and I'm very, very tired of youth and love and self-sacrifice.
—**Bette Davis,** in *Old Acquaintance*

From birth to age eighteen, a girl needs good parents. From eighteen to thirty-five, she needs good looks. From thirty-five to fifty-five, she needs a good personality. From fifty-five on, she needs good cash.
—**Sophie Tucker**

Women are like elephants to me—I like to look at 'em, but I wouldn't want to own one.
—**W. C. Fields**

You know how to whistle, don't you, Steve? You just put your lips together—and *blow*.
—**Lauren Bacall,** in *To Have and Have Not*

Lolita, light of my life, fire of my loins. My sin, my soul. Lo-lee-ta: the tip of the tongue taking a trip of three steps down the palate to tap, at three, on the teeth. Lo. Lee. Ta.
—**Vladimir Nabokov**

I think this is the beginning of a beautiful friendship.
—**Humphrey Bogart,** to Claude Rains in *Casablanca*

I'd love to kiss you, but I just washed my hair.
—**Bette Davis,** in *Cabin in the Cotton*

There are two reasons why I'm in show business, and I'm standing on both of them.
—**Betty Grable**

The average man is more interested in a woman who is interested in him than he is in a woman—any woman—with beautiful legs.
—**Marlene Dietrich**

Good wife best household furniture.
—**Charlie Chan**

I've been in bondage since I was a fetus. . . . I became a thing instead of a person.
—**Judy Garland**

They say a man is as old as the women he feels.
—**Groucho Marx**

I want to be alone.
—**Greta Garbo**

I was going to thrash them within an inch of their lives, but I didn't have a tape measure.
—Groucho Marx

You have courage written all over you. It's the laundry markers, my dear.
—W. C. Fields

Back where I come from, we have men we call heroes. Once a year they take their fortitude out of mothballs to parade it down the main street.
—The Wizard of Oz, to the Cowardly Lion

I stick my neck out for nobody.
—Humphrey Bogart, in Casablanca

Include me out.
—Samuel Goldwyn

If you can't give me your word of honor, will you give me your promise?
—Samuel Goldwyn

Fortunately, assassination of French language not serious crime.
—Charlie Chan

I am only a public entertainer who has understood his time.
—Pablo Picasso

Across an immense ethereal gulf, minds that are to our minds as ours are to the beasts in the jungle—intellects vast, cool, and un-sympathetic—regarded this Earth with envious eyes and slowly and surely drew their plans against us. . . .
—Orson Welles, in the 1938 radio broadcast of The War of the Worlds

I must say I find television very educational. The minute somebody turns it on, I go into the library and read a good book.
—Groucho Marx

I read part of it all the way through.
—Samuel Goldwyn

If at first you don't succeed, try, try again. Then quit. No use being
a damn fool about it.
—**W. C. Fields**

Bad alibi like dead fish—cannot stand test of time.
—**Charlie Chan**

Frankly, my dear, I don't give a damn.
—**Rhett Butler,** to Scarlett O'Hara in *Gone With the Wind*

19
——————————————
High Society

AUGUST 15, 1969, was the date of an historic pilgrimage by Volkswagen vans to the 600-acre holy land: the first living gospel of free love in the green and sun-drenched fields of Woodstock. There, amidst cloudbursts, love bugs, and drugs, a congregation of 400,000 paid homage to the high priests of the "under thirty" generation: Jimi Hendrix, the Jefferson Airplane, Santana, and Janis Joplin.

It was a romantic idyll which degenerated four months later, on December 6, when Mick Jagger and the Rolling Stones led a second—violent—pilgrimage to the Altamont Speedway. Soft drinks were spiked with LSD, and Jagger's haunting "Sympathy for the Devil" signalled the end of a generation—the peace movement shot to hell.

Seven years later, rock and roll rebounded from the underground up onto the dance floor of the local discotheques. There, John Travolta, underscored by the Bee Gees, the Trammps, and K.C. and the Sunshine Band, hustled his way into the hearts of America, along with Donna Summer, Vicki Sue Robinson, and Andy Gibb as the heirs apparent of the second-generation high society.

> We're more popular than Jesus Christ now. I don't know which will go first: rock and roll or Christianity.
> —**John Lennon,** 1966

WIDE WORLD PHOTOS

There are two things John and I always do when we're going to sit down and write a song. First of all we sit down. Then we think about writing a song.
—**Paul McCartney**

Turn on. Tune in. Drop out.
—**Timothy Leary**

I do not take drugs. I am drugs.
—**Salvador Dali**

I have no idea what my public image is and would rather not, you know. 'Cause I got my feet firmly planted in the cheeseburgers, here, man.
—**David Crosby**

I don't know. I don't care. And it doesn't make any difference.
—Jack Kerouac

I wouldn't say I invented tack, but I definitely brought it to its present high popularity.
—Bette Midler

All dancing is a replacement for sex.
—Mick Jagger

Truth is something you stumble into when you think you're going some place else.
—Jerry Garcia

The truth is where the truth is, and it's sometimes in the candy store.
—Bob Dylan

The worst thing a little acid could do to Tricia Nixon is turn her into a merely delightful person instead of a grinning robot.
—Grace Slick

Each trip is just a sidestreet, and before you know it, you're back where you were. Each trip is more disturbing than the one that follows, till eventually the sidestreet becomes a dead end.
—Peter Townshend

We have allowed death to change its name from Southern rope to Northern dope. Too many black youths have been victimized by pushing dope into their veins instead of hope into their brains.
—Reverend Jesse Jackson

I'm the one that's got to die when it's time for me to die, so let me live my life the way I want to.
—Jimi Hendrix

The public hungers to see talented young people kill themselves.
—Paul Simon

Death is when you get sick one day and you don't get well again— can't seem to shake it off.
—John Phillips

> I never hold back, man. I'm always on the outer limits of probability.
> —Janis Joplin

WIDE WORLD PHOTOS

Death is that remedy all singers dream of.
—**Allen Ginsberg**

We're living in a butcher shop. The fact that we die is the only comfort in the whole thing.
—**Leonard Cohen**

Not even boot camp is as tough as being in rock and roll.
—**Patti Smith**

How many roads must a man walk down before you call him a man?
—**Bob Dylan**

It's not only that you can't go home again; you can't pretend to be from a place you only visited.
—**Nat Hentoff**

Music is the glue which has kept this generation from falling apart in the face of incredible adult blindness and ignorance and evilness. It is the new educational system for reform and the medium for revolution.
—**Ralph Gleason**

America is having a nervous breakdown.
—**Allen Ginsberg**

Marty Balin like most geniuses is schizophrenic. Fortunately for us, both of him can sing.
—**David Freiberg,** of the Jefferson Starship

Manic depression has captured my soul.
—**Jimi Hendrix**

Anarchy is the only slight glimmer of hope.
—**Mick Jagger**

My life is a crystal teardrop.
—**Joan Baez**

Sorrow is so easy to express and yet so hard to tell.
—**Joni Mitchell**

Is it true John Denver is splitting up?
—**George Harrison**

I'm leaving the group. I want a divorce.
—**John Lennon,** on the breakup of the Beatles, 1971

The Beatniks and the Beatles are angelic mutations.
—**Salvador Dali**

There's no more rock and roll. It's an imitation. I never did do rock and roll. The Beatles weren't rock and roll, nor the Rolling Stones. Rock and roll ended with Little Anthony and the Imperials.
—**Bob Dylan**

Rock 'n roll is music by the inept for the untutored.
—**Recording executive**

Half the battle is selling music, not singing it. It's the image, not what you sing.
—**Rod Stewart**

The softer you sing the louder you're heard.
—**Donovan**

It was noise, such as the world has rarely heard—absolute caco-phony, metallic, brash, the sound of our age. . . . It hurtled from all sides, from some four hundred amplifiers and was as near total noise as anything I have so far experienced.
—**James Michener,** describing rock music

Punk talks about a new race of beings, beyond gender, sort of like mutant artists, you know. Sort of like art is an anagram for rat. Like these kids are like art rats.
—**Patti Smith,** on punk rock

The typical rock fan isn't smart enough to know when he's being dumped on.
—**Frank Zappa**

Music is the major form of communication. It's the commonest vi-bration, the people's news broadcast.
—**Richie Havens**

Music can measure how broad our horizons are. My mind wants to see to infinity.
—**Stevie Wonder**

Being a singer either creates sexual frustration or stems from it.
—**Terry McEwen,** executive vice president of London Records

I can't get no satisfaction.
—**The Rolling Stones**

Rock and roll is still very much a raunchy, too physical, and unre-fined music. Those who approach it as something more delicate,

artful, or fashionable do so at great risk and danger, because they probably miss it altogether. Rock and roll is not polite. It is rude.
—**Jann Wenner,** editor of *Rolling Stone*

A good rock 'n roll show on any given day could probably outdraw the president.
—**Paul Kantner**

I'm thinking about entering politics. . . . I'd love to do it. But I haven't got the right wife.
—**Mick Jagger**

My attitude is, "Don't give me an award, send me money."
—**Linda Ronstadt**

I consider it my patriotic duty to keep Elvis in the 90-percent tax bracket.
—**Colonel Tom Parker,** when Elvis Presley left for the army

I had to be a millionaire. If I couldn't do it without being crooked, then I'd have to be crooked.
—**John Lennon**

I don't set trends. I just find out what they are and I exploit them.
—**Dick Clark**

All my concerts had no sounds in them: they were completely silent. . . . People had to make their own music in their minds.
—**Yoko Ono**

Audiences don't want to do any work for themselves; they want performers to do everything from blowing up bombs to blowing themselves up, and they just sit there almost into that Orwellian-type thing, zombied out and letting the show do everything.
—**J. Geils Band**

Being an entertainer, especially in times like these, is really a public service.
—**Linda Ronstadt**

It's hard to start out as an entertainer and end up as a person.
—**Joan Baez**

Just because you like my stuff doesn't mean I owe you anything.
—**Bob Dylan**

Probably the biggest bringdown in my life . . . was being in a pop group and finding out just how much it was like everything it was supposed to be against.
—**Mama Cass Elliot**

Success leaves you stranded—in winner's limbo.
—**Papa John Creach**

On stage I make love to twenty-five thousand people; then I go home alone.
—**Janis Joplin**

Everybody else is talking about how hard life is, and here I am singing about how good it is to be alive.
—**John Denver**

[Art is] the reasoned derangement of the senses.
—**Kenneth Rexroth**

Art is the perpetual motion of illusion.
—**Bob Dylan**

Don't try to explain it; just sell it.
—**Motto of Colonel Tom Parker**

Those in the cheaper seats clap. The rest of you rattle your jewelry.
—**John Lennon,** at the Royal Variety Performance in London, November 15, 1963

An encore is like putting an artificial limb on a living body.
—**Keith Jarrett**

People think the Beatles know what's going on. We don't. We're just doing it.
—**John Lennon**

You can destroy your now by worrying about tomorrow.
—**Janis Joplin**

I'm an instant star, just add water and stir.
—**David Bowie**

You can get anything you want at Alice's Restaurant.
—**Arlo Guthrie**

Music is the timeless experience of constant change.
—**Jerry Garcia**

I'm interested in my music lasting only while I'm alive. I'm not writing for the future.
—**Sonny Rollins**

I am interested in anything about revolt, disorder, chaos, especially activity that seems to have no meaning.
—**Jim Morrison**

I searched through rebellion, drugs, diets, mysticism, religions, intellectualism, and much more, only to begin to find . . . that truth is basically simple—and feels good, clean, and right.
—**Chick Corea**

Drugs just accelerate what's going to happen anyway.
—**Keith Richards**

Success is a drug in itself. When you strive to become somebody and you become that person, it's difficult to give it up.
—**Bill Graham,** rock promoter

Marijuana is like Coors beer. If you could buy the damn stuff at a Georgia filling station, you'd decide you wouldn't want it.
—**Billy Carter**

Marijuana will be legal some day, because the many law students who now smoke pot will some day become congressmen and legalize it in order to protect themselves.
—**Lenny Bruce**

Marijuana makes each person God.
—**Jerry Rubin**

No one on earth is more ingenious than an addict out to score.
—Arthur Janov

Chemistry is applied theology.
—August Stanley Owsley II, renowned chemist of Haight Ash-
bury

Reality is just a crutch for people who can't deal with drugs.
—Lily Tomlin

The fun thing about being sober is meeting all the friends I've had
for years—especially the ones I've never met.
—Alice Cooper

You are suggesting I have some sort of romantic attachment. I have
no relationship with her, just a passing acquaintance for two
nights.
—Mick Jagger, on Margaret Trudeau

Anywhere is paradise.
—George Harrison

It is hard to get your thing together if your thing is paradise on
earth.
—Jerry Garcia

I always had a repulsive sort of need to be something more than
human.
—David Bowie

I get into so many genders I couldn't even tell you. I've written from
the mouth of a dog, a horse, dead people, anything. I don't limit
myself.
—Patti Smith

If you swing both ways, you really swing. I just figure, you know,
double your pleasure.
—Joan Baez

Com' on baby, light my fire.
—Jim Morrison

Inside every fat Englishman is a thin Hindu trying to get out.
—**Timothy Leary**

Be careful when you walk on an Oriental carpet because you're stepping on somebody's psychedelic vision.
—**Timothy Leary**

You don't need a weatherman to know which way the wind blows.
—**Bob Dylan** line from which the Weathermen take their name

Bored is stupid.
—**Grace Slick**

Never let go of the fiery sadness called desire.
—**Patti Smith**

If your soul is your belly, nobody can drive you out of your skull.
—**Allen Ginsberg**

No one's free, even the birds are chained to the sky.
—**Bob Dylan**

Nobody ever leaves the bus.
—**Ken Kesey,** motto of the Merry Pranksters

20
"Shrinks"

In the early 1960s, American society experienced a unique coales- cence of events: the breakdown of the family, the growing aware- ness of the effects of unchecked technology on our lives, and the si- multaneous rise in popularity of the psychotherapist. Descended from, but not necessarily loyal to, Freud, the once-rigid discipline of psychiatry expanded into a catalog of different therapies tailored to suit the needs and tastes of troubled Americans. Encounter groups, behavioral and cognitive therapies, sensitivity training, consciousness raising, sexology, and primal scream therapy all of- fered hope. Americans were striving to keep their heads together— sometimes paying fifty dollars or more an hour.

By the 1970s, psychotherapy was such an accepted part of our culture that being an est graduate had become chic, and those who sought professional help were often considered more well adjusted than those who did not. As the divorce rate and alienation of peo- ple from their environment continued to grow, men, women, and children turned in even greater numbers to their shrinks for moral support and love. According to the Report of the President's Com- mission on Mental Health, in 1978 an estimated 21,600,000 to 32,400,000 Americans were receiving some form of therapy. Psy- chology was becoming the new American family.

I've developed a new philosophy. . . . I only dread one day at a
time.
—**Charlie Brown**

One out of four people in this country is mentally imbalanced.
Think of your three closest friends—if they seem okay, then you're
the one.
—**Ann Landers**

You are perfect exactly the way you are.
—**Werner Erhard**

Sometimes I feel like a figment of my own imagination.
—**Lily Tomlin**

I'm complicated, sentimental, lovable, honest, loyal, decent, generous, likeable, and lonely. My personality is not split; it's shredded.
—**Jack Paar**

All of us are crazy in one or another way.
—**Theodore Isaac Rubin**

Any breakdown is a breakthrough.
—**Marshall McLuhan**

Insanity—a perfectly rational adjustment to an insane world.
—**R. D. Laing**

When you look directly at an insane man, all you see is a reflection
of your own knowledge that he's insane, which is not to see him at
all. To see him you must see what he saw.
—**Robert Pirsig**

We cannot unthink unless we are insane.
—**Arthur Koestler**

Sanity is a matter of degree.
—**Aldous Huxley**

At least my neurosis is creative. It could have been writer's block.
—**Woody Allen**

Creativity is neither the product of neurosis nor simple talent, but an intense courageous encounter with the Gods.
—**Rollo May**

Creative minds always have been known to survive any kind of bad training.
—**Anna Freud**

There's no heavier burden than a great potential.
—**Linus**

You don't have to try
You just have to be.
—**David Viscott, M.D.**

One cannot be deeply responsive to the world without being saddened very often.
—**Erich Fromm**

Depression is melancholy minus its charms.
—**Susan Sontag**

Colds, ulcers, flu, and cancer are things we get. Schizophrenic is something we are.
—**Mark Vonnegut**

Not all who would can be psychotic.
—**R. D. Laing**

The biggest big business in America is not steel, automobiles, or television. It is the manufacture, refinement, and distribution of anxiety. It is the only business based on the maxims, "The customer is always wrong," "We aim to displease," and "Send 'em away unhappy."
—**Eric Sevareid**

The patient is always right.
—**Bruno Bettelheim**

Anxiety is the experience of Being affirming itself against Nonbeing.
—**Rollo May**

Stress is the spice of life. . . . Complete freedom from stress is death.
—Hans Selye

I have called the major crisis of adolescence the identity crisis; it occurs in that period of the life cycle when each youth must forge for himself some central perspective and direction, some working unity, out of the effective remnants of his childhood and the hopes of his anticipated adulthood.
—Erik Erikson

Manhood is the ability to outlast despair.
—James Jones

Looking back, my life seems like one long obstacle race, with me as its chief obstacle.
—Jack Paar

Self-pity in its early stage is as snug as a feather mattress. Only when it hardens does it become uncomfortable.
—Maya Angelou

Only the insecure strive for security.
—Wayne Dyer

If life is to be sustained, hope must remain, even where confidence is wounded, trust impaired.
—Erik Erikson

To be is to be vulnerable.
—Norman O. Brown

Our strength is often composed of the weakness we're damned if we're going to show.
—Mignon McLaughlin

I'm cheerful. I'm not happy, but I'm cheerful. There's a big difference. . . . A happy woman has no cares at all; a cheerful woman has cares and learns to ignore that.
—Beverly Sills

Facts do not cease to exist because they are ignored.
—Aldous Huxley

Laughing or crying is what a human being does when there's nothing else he can do.
—**Kurt Vonnegut, Jr.**

I can't live without that blanket. I can't face life unarmed.
—**Linus**

I am more important than my problems.
—**José Ferrer**

Dignity and humility are the cornerstones of compassion. Compassion for myself is the most powerful healer of them all.
—**Theodore Isaac Rubin**

Everybody is his own best physician when it comes to behavior.
—**Hans Selye**

The word "shrink" is good. It shrinks the psychiatrist down to human proportions.
—**Theodore Isaac Rubin**

I do not want anybody to be a Jungian. I want people above all to be themselves.
—**Carl Jung**

Anybody who goes to see a psychiatrist ought to have his head examined.
—**Samuel Goldwyn**

The psychiatrist must become a fellow traveler with his patient.
—**R. D. Laing**

Everyone carries around his own monsters.
—**Richard Pryor**

Words of comfort, skillfully administered, are the oldest therapy known to man.
—**Louis Nizer**

All education today is therapy.
—**Herbert Marcuse**

The only doctor with whom it is expected that you talk about your feelings towards your body is the one who does not handle your body—the psychiatrist.
—**Ellen Frankfort**

Sometimes when I get up in the morning, I feel very peculiar. I feel like I've just got to bite a cat! I feel like if I don't bite a cat before sundown, I'll go crazy! But then I just take a deep breath and forget about it. That's what is known as real maturity.
—**Snoopy**

The essence of greatness is the ability to choose personal fulfillment in circumstances where others choose madness.
—**Wayne Dyer**

He won't get to the root of his problem, because the root of his problem is himself.
—**Carroll O'Connor,** on Archie Bunker

Trouble is the common denominator of living. It is the great equalizer.
—**Ann Landers**

People who fight fire with fire usually end up with ashes.
—**Abigail Van Buren**

Toleration . . . is the greatest gift of the mind; it requires the same effort of the brain that it takes to balance oneself on a bicycle.
—**Helen Keller**

Let us not look back in anger or forward in fear, but around in awareness.
—**James Thurber**

Death is simply a shedding of the physical body, like the butterfly coming out of a cocoon. It is a transition into a higher state of consciousness, where you continue to perceive, to understand, to laugh, to be able to grow, and the only thing you lose is something that you don't need anymore . . . your physical body. It's like putting away your winter coat when spring comes.
—**Elisabeth Kübler-Ross**

Death is not the greatest loss in life. The greatest loss is what dies inside us while we live.
—**Norman Cousins**

Death is psychosomatic.
—**Charles Manson**

Death is evidently not a real tragedy for those who do not feel life.
—**Arthur Janov**

There is no importance in anything save the emotions.
—**William Carlos Williams**

The pain of leaving those you grow to love is only the prelude to an understanding of yourself and others.
—**Shirley MacLaine**

When the satisfaction or the security of another person becomes as significant to one as one's own satisfaction or security, then the state of love exists. . . . Under no other circumstances is a state of love present, regardless of the popular usage of the word.
—**Harry Stack Sullivan**

One ceases to be a child when one realizes that telling one's troubles does not make it any better.
—**Cesare Pavese**

You can almost be certain that the man who commits violent crimes has been treated violently as a child.
—**Karl Menninger**

Violence is the last refuge of the incompetent.
—**Isaac Asimov**

The kindest thing I can say about my childhood is that I survived it.
—**Rubin (Hurricane) Carter**

Give me a child and I'll shape him into anything.
—**B. F. Skinner**

I despair of teaching the ordinary parent how to handle his child.
. . . They have no idea of the proper use of reinforcement. I would
prefer to turn child-raising over to specialists.
—B. F. Skinner

The more people have studied different methods of bringing up
children the more they have come to the conclusion that what good
mothers and fathers instinctively feel like doing for their babies is
the best after all.
—Dr. Benjamin Spock

Wonderful people do not always make wonderful parents.
—Abraham Maslow

Many people who dislike weekends have spent their childhoods in
unhappy homes.
—Theodore Isaac Rubin

Anxious mothers make unsure kids.
—Bruno Bettelheim

There is no failure that can alter the course of human events more
than failing a family.
—Eleanor McGovern

When family relations are no longer harmonious, we have filial
children and devoted parents.
—R. D. Laing

All the advantages of a later life may be wasted on a child who has
lacked a warm and satisfying mother relationship.
—Anna Freud

The two greatest influences in my life have been my parents and
asthma.
—Stanley Siegel

Do not mistake a child for his symptom.
—Erik Erikson

If you're deprived of love when you're young, you can never have it given back to you.
—Jerry Lewis

Loved people are loving people.
—Ann Landers

When you make a world tolerable for yourself, you make a world tolerable for others.
—Anaïs Nin

In life you throw a ball. You hope it will reach a wall and bounce back so you can throw it again. You hope your friends will provide that wall.
—Pablo Picasso

To have no friends at all is the worst state of man. To have only one good friend is enough.
—David Viscott, M.D.

You can make more friends in two months by becoming interested in other people than you can in two years by trying to get other people interested in you.
—Dale Carnegie

Any time friends have to be careful of what they say to friends, friendship is taking on another dimension.
—Duke Ellington

Once you think that your own mind is not your friend anymore . . . you are on your way to insanity.
—Bobby Fischer

The best book for two people to read to improve their love life together is the chronicle of each other's feelings about themselves.
—David Viscott, M.D.

There is an inverse relationship between the number of how-to-do-it books perused by a person, or rolling off the presses in a society, and the amount of sexual passion or even pleasure experienced by the persons involved.
—Rollo May

Take off your shell along with your clothes.
—**Alex Comfort**

The best cure for hypochondria is to forget about your own body and get interested in someone else's.
—**Goodman Ace**

Your sexuality is a dimension of your personality, and whenever you are sexually active, you are expressing yourself—the self that you are at that moment, the mood that you're in, the needs that you have.
—**Virginia Johnson**

Sex is a natural function like breathing or eating.
—**William Masters**

The only unnatural sex act is that which you cannot perform.
—**Alfred Kinsey**

All orgasms are created equal.
—**Dr. David M. Reuben**

Talk between lovers about techniques to improve sex is destructive in bed and constructive out of bed.
—**Theodore Isaac Rubin**

Frigidity is the word used to describe impaired sexual feeling in women . . . and was probably coined by a man.
—**Dr. David M. Reuben**

Sex is the biggest nothing of all time.
—**Andy Warhol**

The only thing age has to do with sex performance is that the longer you love, the more you learn.
—**Alex Comfort**

Our highly vaunted sexual freedom has turned out to be a new form of puritanism. I define puritanism as a state of alienation from the body, separation of emotion from reason, and use of the body as a machine.
—**Rollo May**

Sex ought to be a wholly satisfying link between two affectionate people from which they emerge unanxious, rewarded, and ready for more.
—**Alex Comfort**

Pleasure is not happiness. It has no more importance than a shadow following a man.
—**Muhammad Ali**

The ultimate mystery is one's own self.
—**Sammy Davis, Jr.**

21
"Ford"

AT NOON on August 9, 1974, the day after Richard Nixon resigned, Gerald Ford placed his left hand on the Bible to be sworn in as the thirty-eighth president of this country. In his brief inaugural address, Ford dedicated his administration to healing the wounds of Watergate. A month later, he granted a "full, complete, and absolute" pardon to Richard Nixon.

I am the first Eagle Scout vice president of the United States!
—**Gerald Ford**

Jerry's the only man I ever knew who can't walk and chew gum at the same time.
—**Lyndon Baines Johnson**

How many really intelligent presidents have we had? I think a president has to be able to think like the people think.
—**Betty Ford**

When a man is asked to make a speech, the first thing he has to decide is what to say.
—**Gerald Ford**

It's a little unkind to say about a president of the United States, but Gerald Ford is Charlie McCarthy to Nelson Rockefeller's Edgar Bergen.
—**Robert Welch,** founder of the John Birch Society

I only wish that I could take the entire United States into the locker room at half time. I would simply say that we must look not at the points we have lost but at the points we can gain.
—**Gerald Ford**

Jerry Ford is a nice guy, but he played too much football with his helmet off.
—**Lyndon Baines Johnson**

I don't feel that because I'm First Lady I'm any different from what I was before. It can happen to anyone. After all, it *has* happened to anyone.
—**Betty Ford**

You're very foolish if you try to beat around the bush—you just meet yourself coming around the bush the other way.
—**Betty Ford**

I wouldn't be surprised [if her daughter had an affair]. I think she's a perfectly normal human being like all young girls. If she wanted to continue, I would certainly counsel and advise her on the subject. And I'd want to know pretty much about the young man. . . . She's pretty young to start affairs, [but] she's a big girl.
—**Betty Ford**

The president has long ceased to be perturbed or surprised by his wife's remarks.
—**Ron Nessen,** White House press secretary under Ford

They've asked me everything but how often I sleep with my husband. And if they'd asked me that, I would have told them, "As often as possible."
—**Betty Ford**

66

I'm a very adjustable person. After all, I moved from lawyer to congressman to minority leader to vice president to president without any emotional problems.
—**Gerald Ford**

WIDE WORLD PHOTOS

99

Mr. Chairman, I think the record should show that for the first time since McKinley, we have a Republican president worth shooting, and I think that's a good sign.
—**Representative James P. Johnson,** Republican from Colorado, referring to the attempted assassination of Gerald Ford by Lynette (Squeaky) Fromme

When people around you treat you like a child and pay no attention to the things you say, you have to do something.
—**Lynette (Squeaky) Fromme**

In the current administration, who can use the White House swimming pool and tennis courts is decided at the very highest level. President Ford did not bother himself with such minor details. He let me swim in the pool. He only got upset when I tried to walk across the water.
—**Henry Kissinger,** 1978

Beverly Stills, who can sing everything from Verdi ballads to Strauss operations.
—**Gerald Ford,** introducing opera singer Beverly Sills at the White House

Truth is the glue that holds governments together. Compromise is the oil that makes governments go.
—**Gerald Ford**

A government big enough to give us everything we want would be big enough to take from us everything we have.
—**Gerald Ford**

I'm a Ford, not a Lincoln.
—**Gerald Ford**

Let me call on the real spokesman for the family—Betty.
—**Gerald Ford,** as he conceded defeat to Jimmy Carter in 1975

I'm for women's lib, but I don't mind walking three paces behind Jerry.
—**Betty Ford**

Is there life after the White House?
—**Betty Ford**

22
"Comic Relief"

ON OCTOBER 4, 1961, Lenny Bruce was arrested in San Francisco on obscenity charges—transforming the comedian into a leading spokesman for the Free Speech Movement. Throughout the 1960s, comedy was to become serious business through the hard raps of Dick Gregory, Bill Cosby, and George Carlin. Dick and Tommy Smothers were so trenchant and uncensored in their remarks that CBS bleeped them right off television. Johnny Carson turned his unique sense of social satire into an opening monologue for "The Tonight Show" that tickled the funnybone of Middle America and elevated him into the role of first jester of the tube.

By the 1970s, the *schtiks* of Richard Pryor, Lily Tomlin, and Steve Martin, along with the parodies and slapstick of Woody Allen, Mel Brooks, and Neil Simon had provided a disillusioned generation with a little comic relief.

What you see is what you get.
—**Flip Wilson**

There's a sexual revolution going on, and I think that with our current foreign policy, we'll probably be sending troops in there any minute to break it up.
—**Mel Brooks**

I wasn't as afraid of being killed in battle as I was of being bored.
—**Lenny Bruce**

Thought: Why does man kill? He kills for food. And not only food: frequently there must be a beverage.
—**Woody Allen**

If it weren't for bad luck, I wouldn't have had no luck at all!
—**Dick Gregory**

If anyone drank that much, how long you think people'd keep hirin' him?
—**Dean Martin**

The suburbs were discovered quite by accident one day in the early 1940s by a Welcome-Wagon lady who was lost.
—**Erma Bombeck**

I'll say this about one of us living in an all-white suburb. Crabgrass isn't our biggest problem.
—**Dick Gregory**

My type of person is the one who builds a fallout shelter with a doorbell.
—**Dick Gregory**

He's so snobbish he has an unlisted zip code number.
—**Earl Wilson**

I've got more agents than the IRS.
—**Henny Youngman**

If you're going to do something tonight that you'll be sorry for tomorrow morning, sleep late.
—**Henny Youngman**

I do what I do because I have to get it out. I'm just lucky it wasn't an urge to be a pickpocket. It's an oblique ailment.
—Mel Brooks

It's hard to keep your shirt on when you're getting something off your chest.
—Nipsey Russell

Showing up is 80 percent of life.
—Woody Allen

For fast-acting relief, try slowing down.
—Lily Tomlin

Once there was a time when I thought I could give up thumbsucking. Now I doubt if I ever could. I'm hooked!
—Linus

There are four things that are overrated in this country: hot chicken soup, sex, the FBI, and parking your car in your garage.
—Erma Bombeck

Where humor is concerned, there are no standards—no one can say what is good or bad, although you can be sure that everyone will.
—John Kenneth Galbraith

Humor is just another defense against the universe.
—Mel Brooks

Humor is the most engaging cowardice.
—Robert Frost

Humor is emotional chaos remembered in tranquillity.
—James Thurber

Laughter is the comedian's criterion of talent.
—Jack Paar

Laughter is the shortest distance between two people.
—Victor Borge

Laughter is a response to a gestalt formation where two previously incompatible or dissimilar ideas suddenly form into a new piece of understanding—the energy release during that reaction comes out in laughter.
—**Del Close,** director of Chicago's "Second City"

❝

Laughing is the only form of revolt we have in this country.
—**Larry Klein,** comedy writer for "The Tonight Show"

WIDE WORLD PHOTOS

❞

A middle-class Englishman will assume arrogantly that the English have a monopoly on humor, but he doesn't have the ability to laugh at himself.
—**William David,** editor of *Punch*

Nothing is quite as funny as the unintended humor of reality.
—**Steve Allen**

A humorist is someone who writes with his mouth.
—**Carl Reiner**

Being a comedian is like being a con man. You have to make 'em like you before you can fool 'em.
—**Flip Wilson**

I'm not a comedian. I'm Lenny Bruce.
—**Lenny Bruce**

The role of a comedian is to make the audience laugh, at a minimum of once every fifteen seconds.
—**Lenny Bruce**

A man sufficiently gifted with humor is in small danger of succumbing to flattering delusions about himself, because he cannot help perceiving what a pompous ass he would become if he did.
—**Konrad Lorenz**

Buster Keaton is the father of comedy, Stan Laurel is the son, and Harpo Marx the holy ghost.
—**Marty Feldman**

Funny had better be sad somewhere.
—**Jerry Lewis**

The biggest laughs are based on the biggest disappointments and the biggest fears.
—**Kurt Vonnegut, Jr.**

Happiness is having a scratch for every itch.
—**Ogden Nash**

I have a sixth sense, not the other five. If I wasn't making money they'd put me away.
—**Red Skelton**

If my mind ever listened to what my mouth said, I'd have a lot of accounting to do.
—**Steve Allen**

In the end, everything is a gag.
—**Charlie Chaplin**

23
Tube

TELEVISION'S "VAST WASTELAND" sprouted into a global village in the 1960s when millions of viewers raised the ratings of the Vietnam War by tuning into the guerilla fighting—in the safety of their own bedrooms. With events reeling before the public's eyes, newscasters such as Walter Cronkite, David Brinkley, John Chancellor, and Harry Reasoner were called upon to analyze the news as well as to report it, achieving broad influence as political commentators. In 1968, Vice President Spiro T. Agnew launched a virulent attack against the growing power of the media. Network executives retaliated. The confrontation between news media and government remained a major story for the next four years.

By the 1970s, television news had become a top attraction for the American viewer: Barbara Walters won a million-dollar contract from ABC for her hard-line interviewing, and TV "news magazines"—in-depth investigations of top news items—like "60 Minutes" were vying for ratings with new trends in television entertainment. Norman Lear crispened situation comedies into satires with "All In The Family," its spin-offs "Maude" and "The Jeffersons," and the outrageous mock soap opera "Mary Hartman, Mary Hartman." "Sesame Street" became a regular babysitter during the week, while Mary Tyler Moore became everybody's steady date for Saturday night.

Perhaps, however, it was Fred Silverman, *wunderkind* of all three major netwoks, who most changed the course of TV programming in the 1970s. Silverman introduced nostalgia and a wholesome sexuality in such hits as "Happy Days," "Laverne and Shirley," and "Charlie's Angels" and innovated the new form of mini-series: the adaptation for television of popular novels such as Alex Haley's *Roots*, which drew an estimated 133 million viewers, the highest rating in the history of television.

When television is bad, nothing is worse. I invite you to sit down in front of your television set when your station goes on the air and stay there without a book, magazine, newspaper, profit and loss sheet, or rating book to distract you—and keep your eyes glued to that set until the station signs off. I can assure you that you will observe a vast wasteland.
—**Newton Minow,** in his address to the National Association of Broadcasters, May 9, 1961

Television is: the literature of the illiterate, the culture of the low-brow, the wealth of the poor, the privilege of the underprivileged, the exclusive club of the excluded masses.
—**Lee Loevinger,** former commissioner of the Federal Communications Commission

The instrument can teach, it can illuminate. Yes, and it can even inspire. But it can do so only to the extent that humans are determined to use it to those ends. Otherwise, it is merely lights and wires in a box.
—**Edward R. Murrow**

If you read a lot of books, you're considered well-read. But if you watch a lot of TV, you're not considered well-viewed.
—**Lily Tomlin**

TV—chewing gum for the eyes.
—**Frank Lloyd Wright**

Broadcasting is writing for the mind through the ear.
—**Edward Weeks**

There must be a better way to earn a living than this.
—**Jack Paar,** as he walked off the "Tonight" show in 1960

I hate television. I hate it as much as peanuts. But I can't stop eating peanuts.
—Orson Welles

TV is addictive. It's a drug.
—Marshall McLuhan

There is a young and impressionable mind out there that is very hungry for information. . . . It has latched on to an electronic tube as its main source of nourishment.
Joan Ganz Cooney, creator of "Sesame Street"

Television has changed the American child from an irresistible force into an immovable object.
—Laurence Peter

66

We lost a daughter, Edith, but we gained a meathead!
—Archie Bunker

UNITED PRESS INTERNATIONAL PHOTO

99

Television is a gold goose that lays scrambled eggs; and it is futile
and probably fatal to beat it for not laying caviar.
—**Lee Loevinger**

The ultimate game show will be the one where somebody gets
killed at the end.
—**Chuck Barris,** producer of the "Gong Show"

Television is a superficial medium made so by the short attention
span of a peripatetic audience.
—**Richard Salant,** president, CBS News

Tell 'em not to make the mistakes Hollywood made. . . . Don't start
making shows better after the people have stopped coming.
—**Samuel Goldwyn,** on television

Television has proved that people will look at anything rather than
each other.
—**Ann Landers**

Young man, we have in this country two big television networks.
. . . They're . . . so damned big they think they own the country.
But, young man, don't get any ideas about fighting.
—**Lyndon Baines Johnson,** to Spiro T. Agnew in 1968

It's time we questioned [such power] in the hands of a small and
unelected elite. The great networks have dominated America's air-
waves for decades. The people are entitled to a full accounting of
their stewardship.
—**Spiro T. Agnew,** in his attack against the news media, 1968

Our job is to give people not what they want, but what we decide
they ought to have.
—**Richard Salant,** president, CBS News

Sock-it-to-me.
—**Judy Carne,** on "Laugh-in"

I'm fighting for freedom of the press, and maybe I should also be
fighting for freedom from the press.
—**Daniel Schorr,** after leaking confidential information on CIA
    activities in the Pike Report, in the *Village Voice,* February 23,
    1976

The day when the network commentators and even the gentlemen of the *New York Times* enjoyed a form of diplomatic immunity . . . is over.
—**Spiro T. Agnew,** December 1, 1969

One of these days, Alice, pow—right in the kisser!
—**Ralph Kramden,** on "The Honeymooners"

American journalists today . . . have been forced and lured out of their normal and proper role in our society. They are becoming not just the critics in the aisle but actors in the play.
—**Eric Sevareid**

Today's reporter is forced to become an educator more concerned with explaining the news than with being the first on the scene.
—**Fred Friendly,** paraphrasing James Reston

I now believe in reincarnation. Tonight's monologue is going to come back as a dog.
—**Johnny Carson**

How many marches and demonstrations would we have if the marchers did not know that the ever faithful TV cameras would be there to record their antics?
—**Spiro T. Agnew,** 1969

He who attacks the fundamentals of the American [broadcasting] system attacks democracy itself.
—**William S. Paley,** chairman of the board, CBS

Television is democracy at its ugliest.
—**Paddy Chayefsky**

As human beings, we hope we are up to it; as reporters we hope that we never abuse it.
—**Edward R. Murrow**

He does not speak as much as exhale, and he exhales polysyllabically.
—**Edwin Newman,** on William F. Buckley, Jr.

I don't want to be quoted, and don't quote me that I don't want to be quoted.
—**Winston Burdett,** CBS news correspondent

The prevalence of "Y'know" is one of the most far-reaching and depressing developments of our time.
—**Edwin Newman**

A spirit of national masochism prevails, encouraged by an effete corps of impudent snobs who characterize themselves as intellectuals.
—**Spiro T. Agnew,** in his attack against the news media, November 1969

I hesitate to get into the gutter with this guy.
—**Chet Huntley,** on Spiro T. Agnew

Woe is me . . . because less than 3 percent of you people read books! Because less than 15 percent of you read newspapers! Because the only truth you know is what you get over this tube.
—**Peter Finch,** as Howard Beale, in *Network*

The one function that TV news performs very well is that when there is no news we give it to you with the same emphasis as if there were news.
—**David Brinkley**

Analysis is concerned with things as they are, or as they were, or, judging from present facts, what they probably will be. An editorial is concerned with things as they ought to be.
—**Frank Stanton,** former president, CBS

News analysis is a matter of good judgment and reliance on serious journalists whose restraint you trust.
—**Fred Friendly**

TV news critics are not identified as critics. They're identified as newsmen.
—**H. R. Haldeman**

The real news is bad news.
—**Marshall McLuhan**

And now, in keeping with Channel 40's policy of always bringing you the latest in blood and guts, in living color, you're about to see another first—an attempted suicide.
—**Chris Chubbuck,** TV commentator in Sarasota, Florida, as she shot herself to death on July 15, 1974 while on the air

News isn't news anymore. It's hour-by-hour warnings.
—**Paul Harvey,** ABC news commentator

All news is an exaggeration of life.
—**Daniel Schorr**

Compromise, Tommy, is a way of life. . . . A lack of compromise, you're dead.
—**Dick Smothers,** to his brother Tommy, June 8, 1969, after CBS cancelled their controversial variety show

66

Unless you and I fornicate in front of everybody, people aren't going to think we get along.
—**Barbara Walters,** to co-anchor Harry Reasoner

UNITED PRESS INTERNATIONAL PHOTO

99

Being an anchor is not just a matter of sitting in front of a camera and looking pretty.
—**David Brinkley**

Just be yourself.
—**Hughes Rudd,** to Sally Quinn, as she began her short-lived stint as anchorwoman on the CBS Morning News, July 1973

The only absolute rule is: Never lose control of the show.
—**Johnny Carson**

With rape so predominant in the news lately, it is well to remember the words of Confucius: "If rape is inevitable, lie back and enjoy it."
—**Tex Antoine;** ABC News suspended Antoine for this remark in 1976, and when he returned, he was allowed to work in the WABC weather department but was prohibited from appearing on the air

If there were any medium that should not be concerned with censorship, it should be TV. You have a dial.
—**Burt Reynolds**

The ultimate censorship is the flick of the dial.
—**Tommy Smothers**

My old movies have been on so many channels lately, I can flip the dial and watch the hairline recede.
—**Bob Hope**

What passes for a culture in my head is really a bunch of commercials.
—**Kurt Vonnegut, Jr.**

Television in our country . . . is, even more than movies, the American dream made visible.
—**Irwin Shaw**

Television is going to be the test of the modern world and . . . in this new opportunity to see beyond the range of our vision we shall discover either a new and unbearable disturbance of the general peace or a saving radiance in the sky. We shall stand or fall by television—of that I am quite sure.
—**E. B. White**

24

Hollywood

In 1963, when Twentieth Century Fox sank into the Nile with the film *Cleopatra,* the movie industry shifted from the contract system of the major movie studios to the laissez-faire casting system of the independent filmmakers. With this passage came the end of the star system through which such actors as Elizabeth Taylor, Judy Garland, Mickey Rooney, and Natalie Wood were groomed by the studios from childhood for an adulthood of stardom. Shirley MacLaine became the last contemporary actress to sign a long-term movie contract (with MGM).

Thereafter, hopefuls such as Robert Redford, Faye Dunaway, Dustin Hoffman, Jack Nicholson, and Warren Beatty were obliged to make their own fortunes on the screen. The power in tinseltown had passed from studio moguls to super agents like Sue Mengers, who could command fees of more than a million dollars per picture for her major clients. In the 1970s, as the movie studios became increasingly fossilized, the clout in Hollywood clearly belonged to the superstar.

Reality is a movie.
—Abbie Hoffman

If you stay in Beverly Hills too long you become a Mercedes.
—**Robert Redford**

Success to me is having ten honeydew melons and eating only the top half of each one.
—**Barbra Streisand**

There's no deodorant like success.
—**Elizabeth Taylor**

Hollywood is the only place in the world where an amicable divorce means each one gets 50 percent of the publicity.
—**Lauren Bacall**

Always stay in your own movie.
—**Ken Kesey**

In California everyone goes to a therapist, is a therapist, or is a therapist going to a therapist.
—**Truman Capote**

The world is, for the most part, a collective madhouse, and practically everyone, however "normal" his facade, is faking sanity.
—**John Astin**

If you ask me to play myself, I will not know what to do. I do not know who or what I am.
—**Peter Sellers**

If I seem to be running, it's because I'm pursued.
—**Mia Farrow**

I do twenty minutes every time the refrigerator door opens and the light comes on.
—**Debbie Reynolds**

Reality is something you rise above.
—**Liza Minnelli**

If Solzhenitzyn moved to L.A., within a few months he'd have a hot tub, be doing TM, be writing a movie, and probably have two wives.
—**Paul Mazursky**

As one went to Europe to see the living past, so one must visit Southern California to observe the future.
—**Alison Lurie**

L.A. is a meat factory that grinds people into neat little packages.
—**Keith Moon**

Hollywood is a sewer—with service from the Ritz-Carlton.
—**Wilson Mizner**

Hollywood is like Harvard. Once you're accepted, you can't flunk out.
—**Brandon Tarikoff,** director of comedy at NBC

Beverly Hills is very exclusive. For instance, their fire department won't make house calls.
—**Mort Sahl**

L.A. is my favorite museum.
—**David Bowie**

They say in Hollywood if you want messages you go to Western Union.
—**Marlon Brando**

All creative people should be required to leave California for three months every year.
—**Gloria Swanson**

The only way to avoid Hollywood is to live there.
—**Igor Stravinsky**

Living in L.A. is like not having a date on Saturday night.
—**Candice Bergen**

I've never been out of this country but I've been to California. Does that count?
—**Bob Bergland,** Secretary of Agriculture

I like to work in Hollywood but I don't like to live there. I'm too young to die.
—**Claire Bloom**

In Hollywood success is relative. The closer the relative, the greater the success.
—**Arthur Treacher**

It was no great tragedy being Judy Garland's daughter. I had tremendously interesting childhood years—except they had little to do with being a child.
—**Liza Minnelli**

Success breeds Success.
—**Louise Fletcher**

In the silence of night I have often wished for just a few words of love from one man, rather than the applause of thousands of people.
—**Judy Garland**

Success means never having to admit you're unhappy.
—**Robert Evans**

Hollywood is where if you don't have happiness, you send out for it.
—**Rex Reed**

Hollywood is like an empty wastebasket.
—**Ginger Rogers**

Trash seeks its own level.
—**Celeste** (the former Mrs. John) **Huston**

Two of the cruelest, most primitive punishments our town deals out to those who fall from favor are the empty mailbox and the silent telephone.
—**Hedda Hopper**

In Hollywood, nothing is black or white. Everything is covered with a layer of gray gauze.
—**Peter Bart**

In the frivolous, absurd old days, stars were photographed in their bubble baths; now they bathe in tears of self-pity.
—**Pauline Kael**

Man in the twentieth century has been cut adrift in a rudderless boat on an uncharted sea.
—**Stanley Kubrick**

Hollywood breeds self-contempt. It tells you you're a big star now, here, enjoy, smoke this, snort this, drink this. And you say, "Why not?" But if it all fails tomorrow, that's where suicide comes in.
—**Freddie Prinze**

The drinking is tremendous. . . . At four o'clock, everybody becomes a big martini.
—**Blair Sabol**

It's a hectic, crazy life. You're not like a shoe salesman, who can get rid of his wares. You're stuck with a product—yourself.
—**Nancy Sinatra**

I've always felt that I would never develop into a really fine actress because I cared more about life beyond the camera than the life in front of it.
—**Shirley MacLaine**

The stage is actors' country. You have to get your passport stamped every so often or they take away your citizenship.
—**Charlton Heston**

At one time I thought he wanted to be an actor. He had certain qualifications, including no money and a total lack of responsibility.
—**Hedda Hopper**

An actor . . . is something less than a man, while an actress is something more than a woman.
—**Richard Burton**

When one actor looks into a mirror, that is a love story. When two actors appear on the stage, that is a crime story. Each is trying to steal the show. When one hundred and fifty actors appear on the stage, that is a Billy Rose spectacle.
—Louis Nizer

The great thing about the movies . . . is—you're giving people little . . . tiny pieces of *time* . . . that they never forget.
—James Stewart

My whole life is a movie. It's just that there are no dissolves. I have to live every agonizing moment of it. My life needs editing.
—Mort Sahl

In Hollywood, great actresses are not those actresses who go around trying to find distribution outlets for films on behalf of the Palestine Liberation Organization.
—Vincent Canby

An actor can only hope to be a mirror of humanity, a mirror to be looked into by audiences.
—Shirley MacLaine

All actors are cattle.
—Alfred Hitchcock

Some people claim I say all actors are cattle. What I say is all actors should be treated like cattle.
—Alfred Hitchcock

I'm going to milk those greedy pauses till they're udderless.
—Richard Burton

Working with animals is a lot easier than working with some actors.
—Betty White

Disney, of course, has the best casting. If he doesn't like an actor, he just tears him up.
—Alfred Hitchcock

I would not willingly eat anything that had intelligent life. But I would willingly eat a producer.
—Marty Feldman

I am a sensitive writer, actor, and director. Talking business disgusts me. If you want to talk business, call my disgusting personal manager.
—Sylvester Stallone

If tomorrow I lost my three biggest clients, I'd like to believe that people I consider my friends would still be friends. But I sure wouldn't hear from them as often during the business day.
—Sue Mengers

If someone is dumb enough to offer me a million dollars to make a picture—I am certainly not dumb enough to turn it down.
—Elizabeth Taylor

I've been in trouble all my life, I've done the most unutterable rubbish, all because of money. . . . The lure of the zeros was simply too great.
—Richard Burton

I've never been poor, only broke. Being poor is a frame of mind. Being broke is only a temporary situation.
—Mike Todd

I went into the business for the money, and the art grew out of it. If people are disillusioned by that remark, I can't help it. It's the truth.
—Charlie Chaplin

Hollywood is one big whore.
—Freddie Prinze

I knew her before she was a virgin.
—Oscar Levant, on Doris Day

We all have a contract with the public—in us they see themselves or what they would like to be.
—Clark Gable

In Hollywood all marriages are happy. It's trying to live together afterward that causes problems.
—**Shelley Winters**

The very meaninglessness of life forces a man to create his own meaning.
—**Stanley Kubrick**

Boredom is the midwife of creativity.
—**Talia Shire**

If you use Hollywood as the test tissue for mankind, what could the prognosis be?
—**Pauline Kael**

People have forgotten how to tell a story. Stories don't have a middle or an end any more. They usually have a beginning that never stops beginning.
—**Steven Spielberg**

I'm a Hollywood writer; so I put on a sports jacket and take off my brain.
—**Ben Hecht**

When in doubt, make a western.
—**John Ford**

Westerns are closer to art than anything else in the motion picture business.
—**John Wayne**

Being given good material is like being assigned to bake a cake and having the batter made for you.
—**Rosalind Russell**

Cartoons are the art form of the movie industry I learn most from. . . . Life now is a cartoon. We are cartoons.
—**Richard Pryor**

Laughter is the Vaseline that makes the ideas penetrate better.
—**Lina Wertmuller**

All love scenes started on the set are continued in the dressing room.
—**Alfred Hitchcock**

If you have to kiss somebody at seven AM [on the set], you'd better be friends.
—**Sophia Loren**

I don't say we all ought to misbehave, but we ought to look as if we could.
—**Orson Welles**

Mistresses are more common in California—in fact some of them are very common. It's easier for a man to conceal his mistress there because of the smog.
—**Groucho Marx**

In Hollywood if a guy's wife looks like a new woman—she probably is.
—**Dean Martin**

All marriages that last are with people who do not live in Los Angeles.
—**Farrah Fawcett-Majors**

The only grounds for divorce in California are marriage.
—**Cher**

Love the public the way you love your mother.
—**Maurice Chevalier**

Every time they make a pornographic film, I make money.
—**Walt Disney**

Pornography is not in the hands of the child who discovers his sexuality by masturbating, but in the hands of the adult who slaps him.
—**Bernardo Bertolucci**

My career started ass-backwards.
—**Raquel Welch**

There's more to me than just hair.
—**Farrah Fawcett-Majors**

> Hollywood's a place where they'll pay you a thousand dollars for a kiss, and fifty cents for your soul.
> —**Marilyn Monroe**
>
>
>
> WIDE WORLD PHOTOS

To perceive evil where it exists is, in my opinion, a form of optimism.
—**Roberto Rossellini**

When choosing between two evils, I always like to take the one I've never tried before.
—**Mae West**

Hollywood has been able to get together as many talents as there are in the world—it's destroyed as many.
—**Laurence Harvey**

If it weren't for those friends persuading her to stay in Hollywood, she would still be alive.
—**Joe DiMaggio,** on Marilyn Monroe

You are only a legend when you are dead.
—**Elizabeth Taylor**

They've great respect for the dead in Hollywood, but none for the living.
—**Errol Flynn**

Once in a man's life, for one mortal moment, he must make a grab for immortality; if not, he has not lived.
—**Sylvester Stallone**

Noble acts and momentous events happen in the same way and produce the same impression as the ordinary facts.
—**Roberto Rossellini**

To restore a sense of reality, I think Walt Disney should have a Hardluckland.
—**Jack Paar**

A movie studio is the best toy a boy ever had.
—**Orson Welles**

The camera makes everyone a tourist in other people's reality, and eventually in one's own.
—**Susan Sontag**

Life experiences become acting experiences, which in turn become life experiences.
—**Liv Ullman**

Never let that bastard back in here—unless we need him.
—**Attributed to Adolph Zukor, Samuel Goldwyn, Harry M. Warner,** and others

The creative impetus is with the producers, the practical power is with the directors, but the ultimate power is with the stars.
—**Tony Bill,** producer

I don't want any yes-men around me. I want everyone to tell me the truth—even though it costs him his job.
—**Samuel Goldwyn**

A verbal contract isn't worth the paper it's written on.
—**Samuel Goldwyn**

If there's anything to learn from the history of movies, it's that corruption leads to further corruption, not to innocence.
—**Pauline Kael**

There are never ten ways to do something. Only one. That is a question of morality. You have to be true to yourself and to others.
—**Jeanne Moreau**

The movie business is at the moral level of the South Vietnamese Army.
—**Josh Greenfeld**

Pick your enemies carefully or you'll never make it in Los Angeles.
—**Rona Barrett**

In work, love, and the movies, everything is a fight.
—**Lina Wertmuller**

Directors I can fight. Fires on the set I can fight. Writers, even actors I can fight. But a Jewish colored fellow. This I can't fight.
—**Samuel Goldwyn,** to Sammy Davis, Jr.

If you want something from an audience, you give blood to their fantasies. It's the *ultimate* hustle.
—**Marlon Brando**

The closer we come to the negative, to death, the more we blossom.
—**Montgomery Clift**

Being a movie star is not a purpose.
—**Jane Fonda**

It is more worthwhile to look directly at what is happening, instead of hiding behind morality.
—**Federico Fellini**

I often feel I'll just opt out of this rat race and buy another hunk of Utah.
—**Robert Redford**

My goal is to find the strength to stop acting.
—**Giancarlo Giannini**

I feel like a father toward my old films. You bring children into the world, then they grow up and go off on their own. From time to time you get together, but it isn't always a pleasure to see them again.
—**Michelangelo Antonioni**

We used to have actresses trying to become stars; now we have stars trying to become actresses.
—**Laurence Olivier**

I arrived in Hollywood without having my nose fixed, my teeth capped, or my name changed. That is very gratifying to me.
—**Barbra Streisand**

Only the untalented can afford to be humble.
—**Sylvia Miles**

There are no small parts. Only small actors.
—**Ginger Rogers**

The artist must satisfy his own soul. All you can lose is your reputation.
—**Laurence Harvey**

When I smile, I must also show the grimace behind it.
—**Liv Ullman**

My movies were the kind they show in prisons and airplanes, because nobody can leave.
—**Burt Reynolds**

There's no orphan like the movie that doesn't work; a hit movie has ninety fathers.
—**Ned Tanen,** agent

If you want to do a thing badly, you have to work as hard at it as though you wanted to do it well.
—**Peter Ustinov**

Amateurs hope. Professionals work.
—**Garson Kanin**

I want to build a house with my films. Some of them are the cellar, some are the walls, and some are the windows. But I hope in the end there will be a house.
—**Rainer Werner Fassbinder**

If it can be written, or thought, it can be filmed.
—**Stanley Kubrick**

To shoot a film is to organize an entire universe.
—**Ingmar Bergman**

I'm not a writer. I'm just someone who writes plays and scripts for a single purpose—to serve as skeletons awaiting flesh and sinew.
—**Ingmar Bergman**

Life is a movie. Death is a photograph.
—**Susan Sontag**

Photography is truth. And cinema is truth twenty-four times a second.
—**Jean-Luc Godard**

A photograph can be an instant of life captured for eternity that will never cease looking back at you.
—**Brigitte Bardot**

A movie is like a person. Either you trust it or you don't.
—**Mike Nichols**

It is very rare to find anyone who can become emotionally involved with an abstraction.
—**Stanley Kubrick**

One really only makes one film in his life, and then he breaks it up into fragments and makes it again.
—**Jean Renoir**

The representative form of our time is a remake.
—**Robert Brustein**

Tomorrow is just a fiction of today.
—**Rex Harrison**

Actors don't retire. They just get offered fewer roles.
—**David Niven**

25
"New York"

In february 1975, Mayor Abraham Beame balanced the checking account and realized New York City was verging on bankruptcy. The financial crunch resulted in mass layoffs of municipal workers, depreciation of municipal bonds, and the ever-growing question in the mid-1970s of whether or not metropolitan life in America was going to survive.

Two years later, Mayor Edward Koch vowed not to let the Big Apple grow rotten. Hand in hand with consumer advocate Bess Myerson, Koch cut enough corners to get the city back in shape —with a friendly loan from the federal government in his hip pocket.

Roman Emperor Augustus used to boast that he had found Rome a city of brick and left it a city of marble. Now we, on the contrary, actually are proud to say that we find a city of stone and brick and leave it a city of precast concrete and corrugated tin.
—**Philip Johnson**

New York is the only city in the world where you can get deliberately run down on the sidewalk by a pedestrian.
—**Russell Baker**

The city is an addiction.
—**Timothy Leary**

The city is permanently cruel.
—**Kurt Vonnegut, Jr.**

There's no more crime in New York—there's nothing left to steal.
—**Henny Youngman**

When I left the West Coast I was a liberal. When I landed in New York I was a revolutionary.
—**Jane Fonda**

My first few weeks in New York were an initiation into the kingdom of guts.
—**Shirley MacLaine**

This great, plunging, dramatic, ferocious, swift, and terrible big city is the most folksy and provincial place I have lived in.
—**Alistair Cooke**

Living in New York City gives people real incentives to want things that nobody else wants.
—**Andy Warhol**

I want to go out in a blaze of glory.
—**David ("Son of Sam") Berkowitz**

New York is a place where the rich walk, the poor drive Cadillacs, and beggars die of malnutrition with thousands of dollars hidden in their mattresses.
—**Duke Ellington**

I can hold a note as long as the Chase National Bank.
—**Ethel Merman**

A good loan is better than a bad tax.
—**Robert Wagner**

" New York was something like a circus performer walking a tightrope and juggling at the same time. . . . It could barely maintain its position, but any movement would tip the whole balance.
—**John V. Lindsay**

UNITED PRESS INTERNATIONAL PHOTO "

Where else but in an American democracy could a boy of the lower East Side, born in London to parents fleeing Russian discrimination, grow up to be mayor of a pan-ethnic city?
—**Abraham Beame**

My brother was the athlete. I was always in training to be mayor.
—**Edward Koch**

This muck heaves and palpitates. It is multidirectional and has a mayor.
—**Donald Barthelme**

There is no greenery. It is enough to make a stone sad.
—**Nikita Khrushchev,** during his 1964 visit to New York

If man can live in Manhattan, he can live anywhere.
—**Arthur C. Clarke**

New York is not the cultural center of America, but the business and administrative center of American culture.
—**Saul Bellow**

In Hollywood the favorite word is "sex"; in the Midwest it is "cheese"; in the South, "honey"; in Manhattan, "money."
—**Amy Vanderbilt**

New York is a diamond iceberg floating in river water.
—**Truman Capote**

I dug it, New York City, all—the streets and the snows and the starving and the five-flight walkups and sleeping in rooms with ten people. I dug the trains and the shadows, the way I dug ore mines and coal mines. I just jumped right to the bottom of New York.
—**Bob Dylan**

New York was pandemonium with a big grin on.
—**Tom Wolfe**

New York is a city of terribly lonely people who can get together only when they're drugged or drunk or in bed.
—**Rollo May**

New York has always been an absurd city to live in but, in a perverse sense, this is one of its delights.
—**John Corry**

Lovers in New York don't turn against it . . . because of taxes or crime or decaying public services. They do it because their happiness here is so dependent on illusions, and their illusions collapse.
—**Kurt Vonnegut, Jr.**

If they had as much adultery going on in New York as they said in the divorce courts, they . . . would never have a chance to make the beds at the Plaza.
—**Zsa Zsa Gabor**

I like the rough impersonality of New York. . . . Human relations are oiled by jokes, complaints, and confessions—all made with the assumption of never seeing the other person again.
—**Bill Bradley**

Movement in New York is vertical, horizontal, angular, never casual. In Versailles, you bow; in New York, you dodge cabs.
—**Boris Aronson,** Broadway set designer

The exodus from New York City limits to the suburbs in the last two decades was nothing less than spectacular and probably represents one of the greatest unattended migrations in human history.
—**Dave Marash**

A man who lives in Connecticut and works in New York commonly spends an hour and a half getting to work; he drives from five minutes to half an hour to get to the station; rides from fifty minutes to an hour and twenty minutes on the train; once in New York, he taxis or walks or subways an additional distance before he checks in, frequently already worn out and disgruntled, for what in our civilization is laughingly called a day's work.
—**Harry Reasoner**

It's much better to be a neurotic in New York than in Nashville. There they liked me but they didn't understand me. Here they like me and understand me.
—**Stanley Siegel**

Every true New Yorker believes with all his heart that when a New Yorker is tired of New York, he is tired of life.
—**Robert Moses**

26
"Back to Nature"

In the 1960s, progress backfired in a stream of pollution, resulting in the contamination of the environment and a growing movement to preserve our ecology. Wisconsin Senator Gaylord Nelson's "Earth Day," on April 22, 1970, called national attention to the issue of the environment; champions of the organic garden, such as Euell Gibbons and Adelle Davis, spearheaded a more individual movement back to nature—through your local health-food store. In 1978, there were over 5,000 retail natural-food stores in this country—adding up to a very healthy $700 million-a-year industry.

Supermarkets are all right, but it's much more fun to shop for food in nature.
—**Euell Gibbons**

To single out the most persecuted animal on earth is not easy. Man has persecuted them all, and with almost equal abandon.
—**Cleveland Amory**

Under the philosophy that now seems to guide our destinies, nothing must get in the way of the man with the spray gun.
—**Rachel Carson**

We are indeed much more than what we eat, but what we eat can nevertheless help us to be much more than what we are.
—**Adelle Davis**

Degrees of sugar abuse and sugar blues vary. However, the body does not lie. If you take sugar, you feel the consequences.
—**William Dufty**

If God meant us to eat sugar he wouldn't have invented dentists.
—**Ralph Nader**

All tastes are acquired tastes. We are born with a taste for nothing except human milk.
—**Euell Gibbons**

Obesity is a war, and we who are fighting it daily are well aware of the turmoil and strain of battle.
—**Jean Nidetch,** founder of Weight Watchers

If we now consider typical American meals with a critical eye, we see innocent stupidity elevated to an art.
—**Adelle Davis**

People who take an optimum amount of vitamin C will experience only a quarter as much illness as those who don't. Through proper use, we could raise the average life expectancy by eight years.
—**Linus Pauling**

In every case, vitamin C appears to be the good Christian ready to soothe the aching brow.
—**Adelle Davis**

Vegetables are interesting but lack a sense of purpose when unaccompanied by a good cut of meat.
—**Fran Lebowitz**

We make ourselves sick by worrying about our health.
—**Dr. Lewis Thomas**

Every day you do one of two things: build health or produce disease in yourself.
—**Adelle Davis**

Thousands upon thousands of persons have studied disease. Almost no one has studied health.
—**Adelle Davis**

The great secret, known to internists and learned early in marriage by internists' wives, but still hidden from the general public, is that most things get better by themselves. Most things, in fact, are better by morning.
—**Dr. Lewis Thomas**

How much health care Americans get should depend not on how much they can afford but on how much they need.
—**Edward M. Kennedy**

I am just a simple doctor. All I wanted to do here was to found a small hospital.
—**Albert Schweitzer**

You can say this for these ready-mixes—the next generation isn't going to have any trouble making pies exactly like mother used to make.
—**Earl Wilson**

Ignorance is a challenge to the nutritionist, but what does one do about opinionated ignorance?
—**Carleton Fredericks**

We have probed the earth, excavated it, burned it, ripped things from it, buried things in it. . . . That does not fit my definition of a good tenant. If we were here on a month-to-month basis, we would have been evicted long ago.
—**Rose Elizabeth Bird,** first woman chief justice of California

Pollution is nothing but resources we're not harvesting.
—**R. Buckminster Fuller**

Nature does have manure and she does have roots as well as blossoms, and you can't hate the manure and blame the roots for not being blossoms.
—**R. Buckminster Fuller**

The faces of the past are like leaves that settle to the ground. . . . They make the earth rich and thick, so that new fruit will come forth every summer.
—**Chief Dan George**

Evolution has her own accounting system and that's the only one that matters.
—**R. Buckminster Fuller**

The sea is not a bargain basement. . . . The greatest resource of the ocean is not material but the boundless spring of inspiration and well-being we gain from her. Yet we risk poisoning the sea forever just when we are learning her science, art, and philosophy and how to live in her embrace.
—**Jacques Cousteau**

Biological sciences will in the end take the lead, for without life, there is no science.
—**Jacques Cousteau**

Ecology has become the political substitute for the word "mother-hood."
—**Jesse Unruh**

To enter life by way of the vagina is as good a way as any.
—**Henry Miller**

The mother of the year should be a sterilized woman with two adopted children.
—**Paul Ehrlich**

It is better that the mother discover her child by touching it. Better to feel before she sees. Better to sense this warm and trembling life, to be moved in her heart by what her *hands* tell her. To hold her child rather than merely look at it.
—**Dr. Frederick Leboyer**

The baby should be addressed in its *own* language. The language that precedes words.
—**Dr. Frederick Leboyer**

If you've seen one redwood, you've seen them all.
—**Ronald Reagan**

We have to face the fact that one day humanity *will* disappear. There is no escaping that fact. The question is, when?
—**Richard Leakey**

There can be no double standard. We cannot have peace among men whose hearts find delight in killing any living creature.
—**Rachel Carson**

In spite of chain-smoking Pall Malls since I was fourteen, I think my wind is still good enough for me to go chasing after happiness.
—**Kurt Vonnegut, Jr.**

A dog is an existentialist. . . . An ill behaved dog in any category, though, is a human failing.
—**Roger Caras**

To his dog, every man is Napoleon, hence the popularity of dogs.
—**Aldous Huxley**

No piano ever lay with crossed paws and saddened eyes on his master's grave.
—**Roger Caras**

A nose that can see is worth two that sniff.
—**Eugene Ionesco**

Killing an animal to make a coat is a sin.
—**Doris Day**

It's a very selfish decade. It's all *me*. People who experienced profound disappointment trying to change the system are jogging and growing vegetables and concentrating on brightening their corner of the world.
—**Tom Hayden**

Come and visit us again. . . . But for heaven's sake, don't come here to live.
—**Tom McCall,** former governor of Oregon

Diet—a system of starving yourself to death so you can live a little longer.
—**Totie Fields**

Diet is a way of eating for the kind of life you want.
—**Helena Rubenstein**

Diets are for those who are thick and tired of it.
—**Mary Tyler Moore**

Don't put off for tomorrow what you can reduce today.
—**Dr. Irwin M. Stillman**

Becoming plump is routine for a woman: she just fills out a form.
—**Earl Wilson**

I am not a glutton—I am an explorer of food.
—**Erma Bombeck**

There are an awful lot of skinny people in the cemetery.
—**Beverly Sills**

A good diet can cure many of the world's ills.
—**Dr. Robert Atkins**

To say that obesity is caused merely by consuming too many calories is like saying that the only cause of the American Revolution was the Boston Tea Party.
—**Adelle Davis**

The other day I got on a weighing machine that stamps your weight on a card. When the card came out, it said, "Come back in ten minutes—alone."
—**Jackie Gleason**

No person should be denied equal rights because of the shape of her skin.
—**Pat Paulsen**

You know you've reached middle age when your weightlifting consists merely of standing up.
—**Bob Hope**

The body is a test tube. You have to put in exactly the right ingredients to get the best reaction out of it.
—Jack Youngblood

I take a tremendous amount of vitamins, which includes a giant Swiss pill each morning, and six protein-rich pony pills—what's good for a horse is good for people.
—Diana Vreeland

Men of the future—perhaps very soon—can live as fishes!
—Jacques Cousteau

66

Life is an error-making and an error-correcting process, and nature in marking man's papers will grade him for wisdom as measured both by survival and by the quality of life of those who survive.
—Jonas Salk

UNITED PRESS INTERNATIONAL PHOTO

99

Every mystery solved brings us to the threshold of a greater one.
—**Rachel Carson**

Unfortunately, unlike bones, behavior does not become fossilized.
—**Richard Leakey**

As for man . . . he doesn't even consider himself an animal—
which, considering the way he considers them, is probably, all
things considered, the only considerate thing about him.
—**Cleveland Amory**

The perils of duck hunting are great, especially for the duck.
—**Walter Cronkite**

27
"
Gurus
"

IN THE 1960s, the expanded awareness of the American student rebelled against the confines of a traditional university education. Stripped of their parents' values and middle-class ideals by Timothy Leary and the Rolling Stones, the younger generation buried the Greek philosophers in their libraries and followed Maharishi Mahesh Yogi, Baba Ram Dass, and the Maharaj Ji. Every self-respecting youth had his own guru to lead him down the primrose path to the divine light. By the 1970s, the university without walls had become a reality. True knowledge was sought through cross-legged meditation in one's own living room.

The essence of Camp is its love of the unnatural, of artifice and exaggeration. . . . Camp asserts . . . that there exists, indeed, a good taste of bad taste.
—Susan Sontag

A country without intellectuals is like a body without a head.
—Ayn Rand

The intellectual life is about your feelings. It's a state of being active with your consciousness responding to your environment.
—Susan Sontag

Being an intellectual creates a lot of questions and no answers. You can fill your life up with ideas and still go home lonely. All you really have that really matters are feelings.
—Janis Joplin

I exist because I think.
—Jean-Paul Sartre

The only thing that Jean-Paul Sartre and I have in common is that he overtips and I over tip.
—Woody Allen

Our ability to speak is just one aspect of the evolutionary drive to create a more accurate world in our heads.
—Richard Leakey

"

Language is a form of organized stutter.
—Marshall McLuhan

HARRY BENSON, PEOPLE WEEKLY © 1978 TIME INC.

"

The purely abstract theorist runs the risk that, as with modern decor, the furniture of his mind will be sparse, bare, and uncomfortable.
—Robert Merton

To expect truth to come from thinking signifies that we mistake the need to think with the urge to know.
—Hannah Arendt

Great minds struggle to cure diseases so that people may live longer, but only madmen ask why. One lives longer in order that he may live longer. There is no other purpose.
—Robert Pirsig

Freedom from the desire for an answer is essential to the understanding of a problem.
—J. Krishnamurti

The external harmony and progress of the entire human race is founded on the internal harmony and progress of every individual.
—Maharishi Mahesh Yogi

The idea of progress is not merely a dream unfulfilled but an inherent absurdity.
—Philip Slater

The absurd is the essential concept and the first truth.
—Albert Camus

What we call progress is the exchange of one nuisance for another nuisance.
—Havelock Ellis

Progress might have been all right once, but it's gone on too long.
—Ogden Nash

The danger of the past was that men became slaves. The danger of the future is that men may become robots.
—Erich Fromm

People have to make themselves predictable, because otherwise the machines get angry and kill them.
—Gregory Bateson

The ordinary affairs of men proceed if they do not always progress.
—Eric Sevareid

Consciousness = energy = love = awareness = light = wisdom = beauty = truth = purity. It's all the SAME. Any trip you want to take leads to the SAME place.
—Baba Ram Dass

The truth believed is a lie. If you go around preaching the truth, you are lying. The truth can only be experienced.
—Werner Erhard

Unreality is the true source of powerlessness. What we do not understand, we cannot control.
—Charles Reich

It should be possible to explain the laws of physics to a barmaid.
—Albert Einstein

Future freedom has no reality; it is only an idea. Reality is what is.
—J. Krishnamurti

It's co-existence or no existence.
—Bertrand Russell

Humanity is acquiring the right technology for all the wrong reasons.
—R. Buckminster Fuller

Man has lost the capacity to foresee and to forestall. He will end by destroying the earth.
—Albert Schweitzer

To a man wielding a microscope, his own seeing eyes are blind.
—Susan Sontag

Society does not understand nature.
—R. Buckminster Fuller

We can destroy ourselves by cynicism and disillusion, just as effectively as by bombs.
—Kenneth Clark

To have arrived on this earth as the product of a biological accident, only to depart through human arrogance, would be the ultimate irony.
—Richard Leakey

It is a well-known fact that we always recognize our homeland at the moment we are about to lose it.
—Albert Camus

We should now give some real thought to the possibility of reforming our technology in the directions of smallness, simplicity, and nonviolence.
—E. F. Schumacher

Civilization can be defined at once by the basic questions it asks and by those it does not ask.
—André Malraux

What I want is some assurance before I die that the human race will be allowed to continue.
—Bertrand Russell

Life is bliss; no person need suffer anymore.
—Maharishi Mahesh Yogi

Every soul speaks the same language. Know that language of love which swells within the human temple.
—Maharaj Ji

Those who say life is worth living at any cost have already written for themselves an epitaph of infamy, for there is no cause and no person they will not betray to stay alive.
—Sidney Hook

It does not do to leave a live dragon out of your calculations, if you live near him.
—J. R. Tolkien

It is better to be a live jackal than a dead lion—for jackals, not men.
—Sidney Hook

The game is not about becoming somebody, it's about becoming nobody.
—Baba Ram Dass

To be born is to die.
—Norman O. Brown

In three words I can sum up everything I've learned about life. It goes on.
—Robert Frost

It is easier to love humanity as a whole than to love one's neighbor.
—Eric Hoffer

Hell is—other people.
—Jean-Paul Sartre

From family to nation, every human group is a society of island universes.
—Aldous Huxley

Small is beautiful.
—E. F. Schumacher

The faces of men, while sheep in credulity, are wolves for conformity.
—Carl Van Doren

We must have respect for both our plumbers and our philosophers or neither our pipes or our theories will hold water.
—John W. Gardner

Belief is a disease.
—Werner Erhard

A belief system is myth, created by knowledge or data without experience. If you experience something, it is real for you, and if you communicate it to somebody, it's real for them. If they now tell it to somebody else, it's a lie—belief without the component of experience.
—Werner Erhard

One man's taboo is another man's charisma.
—Herman Kahn

Charisma means looking like everyone else.
—Marshall McLuhan

The state of enchantment is one of certainty. When enchanted, we neither believe nor doubt nor deny: we know, even if . . . our knowledge is self-deception.
—W. H. Auden

Man is unique among animals in his practiced ability to know things that are not so.
—Philip Slater

When wisdom and sagacity arise, there are great hypocrites.
—R. D. Laing

Don't despise hypocrites too much. See through them. They are sometimes a sign of what we should like to be.
—C. P. Snow

Passionate hatred can give meaning and purpose to an empty life.
—Eric Hoffer

The purpose of life is the expansion of happiness.
—Maharishi Mahesh Yogi

Life is not complete till you acquire a master.
—Shri Satyapal Ji

A new idea is a light that illuminates presences which simply had no form for us before the light fell on them.
—Susanne K. Langer

Many creatures have brains. Man alone has mind.
—R. Buckminster Fuller

Mind is like an ocean. The surface layers of the mind function actively while the deeper levels remain silent.
—Maharishi Mahesh Yogi

The study of the art of motorcycle maintenance is really a miniature study of the art of rationality itself. . . . The motorcycle is primarily a mental phenomenon.
—Robert Pirsig

No sense makes sense.
—Charles Manson

The transcendental state of Being lies beyond all seeing, hearing, touching, smelling, and tasting—beyond all thinking and beyond all feeling.
—Maharishi Mahesh Yogi

Sleep is a state of equilibrium, a kind of monster in which your body disappears. Nothing is left then but the head supported by a subtle host of crutches. . . . It is only when all the crutches are balanced . . . that the god of sleep can take possession of you.
—Salvador Dali

We take a handful of sand from the endless landscape of awareness around us and call that handful of sand the world.
—Robert Pirsig

Time is not the fourth dimension, and should not be so identified. Time is only a relative observation.
—R. Buckminster Fuller

Time talks. It speaks more plainly than words. . . . It can shout the truth where words lie.
—Edward Hall

If we are honest we have to admit that we will never fully know what happened to our ancestors in their journey towards modern humanity.
—Richard Leakey

The white race is the cancer of history.
—**Susan Sontag**

Archaeology cannot altogether transcend the fact that it is based on human garbage.
—**Philip Slater**

Mr. and Mrs. America—you are wrong. I am not the king of the Jews nor am I a hippie cult leader. I am what you have made of me and the mad dog devil killer friend leper is a reflection of your society. . . . Whatever the outcome of this madness that you call a fair trial or Christian Justice, you can know this: In my mind's eye my thoughts light fires in your cities.
—**Charles Manson**

Truth is error burned up.
—**Norman O. Brown**

I am not of your world. I've spent all my life in prison when I was a child. I was an orphan and too ugly to be adopted. Now I am too beautiful to be set free.
—**Charles Manson**

History is the refusal to "let the dead bury their dead."
—**Alan Watts**

History is a kind of Marat/Sade of the human race—a diary kept by narcissists, about narcissists, and largely for narcissists.
—**Philip Slater**

You don't change the course of history by turning the faces of portraits to the wall.
—**Jawaharlal Nehru**

People can cry much easier than they can change.
—**James Baldwin**

The most distinguished hallmark of the American society is and always has been—change.
—**Eric Sevareid**

Americans are trained from infancy for mutationhood.
—**Philip Slater**

Experience is not what happens to a man. It is what a man does with what happens to him.
—**Aldous Huxley**

The basic fact of today is the tremendous pace of change in human life.
—**Jawaharlal Nehru**

Western civilization is a man running with increased speed through an air-sealed tunnel in search of additional oxygen.
—**Philip Slater**

The pace of events is moving so fast that unless we can find some way to keep our sights on tomorrow, we cannot expect to be in touch with today.
—**Dean Rusk**

There is more to life than increasing its speed.
—**Mahatma Gandhi**

Every society faces not merely a succession of probable futures, but an array of possible futures, and a conflict over preferable futures.
—**Alvin Toffler**

We march backwards into the future.
—**Marshall McLuhan**

Future shock is the dizzying disorientation brought on by the premature arrival of the future.
—**Alvin Toffler**

Future shock is the human response to overstimulation.
—**Alvin Toffler**

We may define future shock as the distress, both physical and psychological, that arises from an overload of the human organism's physical adaptive systems and its decision-making processes.
—**Alvin Toffler**

The world is before you, and you need not take it or leave it as it was when you came in.
—**James Baldwin**

All movements go too far.
—**Bertrand Russell**

Man is a luxury-loving animal. His greatest exertions are made in pursuit not of necessities but of superfluities.
—**Eric Hoffer**

An ambitious man can never know peace.
—**J. Krishnamurti**

A person can think and meditate better if he is always a little hungry, never quite warm enough, and never falling prey to the dangers of the soft life of self-gratification.
—**Shirley MacLaine**

Meditation is just oiling the machinery and making the unused parts come into use.
—**Maharishi Mahesh Yogi**

You have not done enough, you have never done enough, so long as it is possible that you have something of value to contribute.
—**Dag Hammarskjöld**

Civilization begins with order, grows with liberty, and dies with chaos.
—**Will Durant**

Do not seek death. Death will find you. But seek the road which makes death a fulfillment.
—**Dag Hammarskjöld**

28
66―――――――――――――――――――――――――――――"
Spirit

ATTENDANCE LEVELS at church were sinful, but on street corners throughout the country the Hare Krishna were recruiting new members with astonishing ease. Though traditional churches were divided over increasingly liberal doctrines—oral contraceptives, women priests, the Charismatic Movement—the Reverend Sun Myung Moon brought it all together with his Unification Church. As parents despaired over this alarming turn of events, Ted Patrick made a career of recapturing and deprogramming their Moon-struck children.

Technology added a new dimension to the spiritual life of Americans with the advent of the televised sermon—the gospel according to the Reverend Ike, Dr. Robert Schuller, Oral Roberts, and others. Ruth Carter Stapleton, however, proved the apostle of the decade when she converted hustler Larry Flynt to Christian morality!

―――――――――――――

Let's all give God a great big hand.
—Reverend Ike

No one would have been invited to dinner as often as Jesus was unless he were interesting and had a sense of humor.
—Charles Schultz

> Jesus Christ is who's great, little girl. I knew that long before them rock and roll freaks made Him a "superstar."
> —Archie Bunker

WIDE WORLD PHOTOS

I do benefits for all religions; I'd hate to blow the hereafter on a technicality.
—Bob Hope

The Unification Church is not another denomination. It is an effort to save the world.
—Reverend Sun Myung Moon

God is a God of love. But Moon doesn't teach you anything except to hate. Hate your mother and father. Hate your brother. Hate food. Hate sex. Hate your school. Hate your government. Your face is just filled with hate. That's Satan.
—Ted Patrick, deprogrammer, to followers of Reverend Sun Myung Moon

The word of the Lord falls with the force of a snowflake.
—Reverend William Sloane Coffin

Why is it when we talk to God, we're said to be praying—but when God talks to us, we're schizophrenic?
—Lily Tomlin

The only complete love is for God. The goal is to love everyone equally, but it doesn't necessarily work out that way.
—George Harrison

The lion and the calf shall lie down together but the calf won't get much sleep.
—**Woody Allen**

I don't love humanity. I don't hate them either. I just don't know them personally.
—**Alan Arkin**

People are too good for this world.
—**Kurt Vonnegut, Jr.**

I don't see myself as a preacher on television at all. . . . I see myself as a doctor in an emergency ward, and those people who are flipping their dials are in pain and dying. . . . I heal through offering what America needs on TV—a philosophy of self-esteem that will make us great once more.
—**Dr. Robert Schuller,** the original Orange County drive-in preacher

Although the world is very full of suffering, it is also full of the overcoming of it.
—**Helen Keller**

The poor may inherit the earth, but it will appear that the rich . . . will inherit the church.
—**Reverend James A. Pike**

Vow and pay, vow and pay, the scripture does say, vow and pay.
—**Brother Don Stewart**

The church is the only business that picks up during bad times.
—**Reverend Charles Angel,** associate minister of the All-Black Tabernacle Church

Frying is like baptism in certain religious sects—there must be total immersion.
—**James Beard**

I'm not OK—you're not OK, and that's OK.
—**Reverend William Sloane Coffin**

Americans are so tense and keyed up that it is impossible even to put them to sleep with a sermon.
—**Norman Vincent Peale**

Boredom is rage spread thin.
—**Paul Tillich**

The Christian life is not a way "out" but a way "through" life.
—**Reverend Billy Graham**

I don't believe in an afterlife, although I am bringing a change of underwear.
—**Woody Allen**

The absurd is sin without God.
—**Albert Camus**

Religion is a feeble attempt to share the sense of God.
—**John Denver**

Religion is just a whole sexual sublimation.
—**Viva**

A person guilty of rape should be castrated. That would stop him pretty quick.
—**Reverend Billy Graham**

What nuns don't realize is that they look better in nun clothes than J. C. Penney pantsuits.
—**Walker Percy**

When I was a small boy . . . I searched the heavens for a miracle. Since then I tried to find the miracle through my art. Now I know that the miracle is Israel.
—**Marc Chagall**

Elsewhere you die and disintegrate. Here you die and mingle.
—**Saul Bellow,** on Israel

Spiritually and culturally to be a Jew is to be a man on the road from Jerusalem to Jerusalem.
—**Theodore Bikel**

I'm sure Christ wore a mezuzah. He certainly didn't wear a cross.
—**Cesar Chavez**

To step on a rabbi's foot . . is a sin, according to the Torah, comparable to the fondling of matzos with any intent other than eating them.
—Woody Allen

Gentiles have a different way of suffering. They suffer without neuroses.
—Henry Miller

Look at Jewish history. Unrelieved lamenting would be intolerable. So, for every ten Jews beating their breasts, God designated one to be crazy and amuse the breast-beaters. By the time I was five I knew I was that one.
—Mel Brooks

Sin is a disproportionate seriousness.
—Bishop Fulton J. Sheen

There are only three sins—causing pain, causing fear, causing anguish. The rest is window dressing.
—Roger Caras

Your cravings as a human animal do not become a prayer just because it is God whom you ask to attend to them.
—Dag Hammarskjöld

The Lord may not come when you want him, but he's always going to be there on time.
—Lou Gossett, Jr.

You people ought to stop all this kneeling down to pray. When you kneel, you're in a perfect position for somebody to kick you right in the behind.
—Reverend Ike

Respect is what we owe; love is what we give.
—Jeane Dixon

God may help those who help themselves, but the courts are rough as hell on shoplifters.
—Leo Rosten

A life that is not open to the holy is not only unworthy of spirit, it is unworthy of life.
—**Martin Buber**

Got no religion. Tried a bunch of different religions. The churches are divided. Can't make up their minds and neither can I.
—**Bob Dylan**

The Good Shepherd is always in search of the lost sheep.
—**Bishop Fulton J. Sheen**

If God did not exist, we should have to invent Him. If God did exist, we should have to abolish Him.
—**Albert Camus**

God loves all men, but is enchanted by none.
—**Isaac Asimov**

God invented man, and man invented the metric system. So to get an image of God all I need is to photograph a perfect man and a precise meter.
—**Salvador Dali**

Man is a greater miracle than any god he ever invented.
—**Rod Steiger**

Every man would like to be God, if it were possible; some few find it difficult to admit the impossibility.
—**Bertrand Russell**

It is the final proof of God's omnipotence that he need not exist in order to save us.
—**Peter De Vries**

I could prove God statistically.
—**George Gallup, Jr.**

I fall back on God, if only out of a desire to trample my doubts underfoot.
—**E. M. Cioran**

Perhaps God is not dead: perhaps God is Himself mad.
—R. D. Laing

God has never explained to man the secret of physical birth—then why should we hesitate to accept the birth of the spiritual man? Both come from God.
—Kathryn Kuhlman

A thick skin is a gift from God.
—Konrad Adenauer

Why would we have different races if God meant us to be alike and associate with each other?
—Lester Maddox

66

Had I gone my own way and not gotten to know God or accepted Him as a part of my life, I think that I would have been a very belligerent individual, full of hate and bitterness.
—Anita Bryant

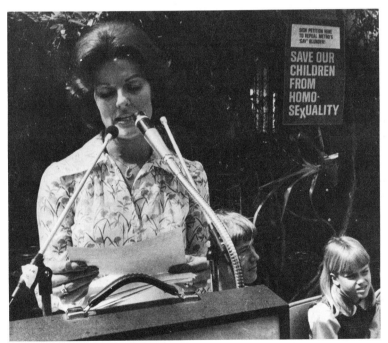

UNITED PRESS INTERNATIONAL PHOTO

99

The price of hating other human beings is loving oneself less.
—**Eldridge Cleaver**

I don't hate homosexuals. I love homosexuals. It's the sin of homo-sexuality I hate.
—**Anita Bryant**

All illness comes from sin. This everyone must take, whether they like it or not; it comes from sin—whether it be of body, of mind, or of soul.
—**Edgar Cayce**

The essence of religiousness is to break rules at the proper time.
—**Harold Jackson,** district attorney at the Milwaukee Twelve trial, 1969

If a man is called to be a streetsweeper, he should sweep streets even as Michelangelo painted, or Beethoven composed music, or Shakespeare wrote poetry. He should sweep streets so well that all the host of heaven and earth will pause to say, here lived a great streetsweeper who did his job well.
—**Dr. Martin Luther King, Jr.**

Work is the Protestant ethic? I think of it as Jewish.
—**Edward Koch**

By perseverance the snail reached the Ark.
—**Charles Spurgeon**

In our era, the road to holiness necessarily passes through the world of action.
—**Dag Hammarskjöld**

You cannot have faith without results any more than you can have motion without movement.
—**Kathryn Kuhlman**

I just want to lobby for God.
—**Reverend Billy Graham**

I'm a candidate for no office but heaven and I have no Republican opposition.
—Sam Ervin

God was my campaign manager.
—Lester Maddox

The majority of believers have belief without understanding.
—Mick Jagger

An atheist is a man who watches a Notre Dame-SMU football game and doesn't care who wins.
—Dwight D. Eisenhower

An atheist is a man who has no invisible means of support.
—Bishop Fulton J. Sheen

I was an atheist. Then I became a Christian. Then I became a born-again Christian, and now I have become a Christian patriot. And all that happened in a two-week period.
—Larry Flynt

If Jesus loves Larry Flynt, who am I to turn my back?
—Ruth Carter Stapleton

Faith is that quality or power by which the things desired become the things possessed.
—Kathryn Kuhlman

When a man is drowning, it may be better for him to try to swim than to thrash around waiting for divine intervention.
—Reverend William Sloane Coffin

It was an act of God.
—Charles F. Luce, chairman of Consolidated Edison Company, explaining the New York blackout, July 14, 1977

The difference between the pessimist and the cynic is that the pessimist carries on the losing battle against life in his own soul, while the cynic tries to wage the battle in someone else's soul.
—Bishop Fulton J. Sheen

A real Christian is a person who can give his pet parrot to the town gossip.
—**Reverend Billy Graham**

Hell is full of noise and is probably full of clocks that emphasize the time that never passes.
—**Bishop Fulton J. Sheen**

I've read the last page of the Bible. It's all going to turn out all right.
—**Reverend Billy Graham**

Do not wait for the last judgment. It takes place every day.
—**Albert Camus**

29
66

Politics

99

IN THE 1960s and the early 1970s, American politics were infused
with the spirit of the new humanism that had first been espoused
by John and Robert Kennedy and Lyndon Baines Johnson. Politicians such as Eugene McCarthy, Edmund Muskie, Fred Harris,
George McGovern, and others gained prominence with platforms
that offered hope for a new society—joining together our diverse
racial, ethnic, and political groups to "form a more perfect union."
This political philosophy peaked in the July 12th, 1972 nomination
of George McGovern for president—by a liberal delegation with a
marked rise in representation among women, students, and blacks.
McGovern's strong convictions against the war in Vietnam had won
him loyal support, but his choice of Thomas Eagleton as a running
mate, his failure to project a strong image to the American voters,
and the difficulty of unseating the incumbent (Richard Nixon) defeated him at the polls.

Nixon's victory against McGovern—the greatest landslide in
American history—reversed the 1960s' trend, turning the sights of
war-weary Americans homeward. By 1974, when Nixon resigned
over the Watergate scandal, disillusioned Americans had yet another series of crises to face. The energy crunch, unemployment,
and runaway inflation had become the primary concerns. No longer
were the masses crusading together; feelings of isolationism and

concern for one's own welfare were now shaping the nation's political mood.

There cannot be a crisis next week. My schedule is already full.
—**Henry Kissinger**

> I can't type. I can't file. I can't even answer the phone.
> —**Elizabeth Ray**

WIDE WORLD PHOTOS

I was never worried about any sex investigation in Washington. All the men on my staff can type.
—**Bella Abzug**

Washington appears to be filled with two kinds of politicians—those trying to get an investigation started, and those trying to get one stopped.
—**Earl Wilson**

Every so often, we pass laws repealing human nature.
—**Howard Lindsay** and **Russel Crouse**

I know you will vote for me until I die. And even after I'm dead I think some of you will write my name in.
—**Adam Clayton Powell**

The mark of a good politician is the ability to stop at two drinks.
—**Charles Colson,** quoting Richard Nixon's adage

The difference between the men and the boys in politics is, and always has been, that the boys want to be something, while the men want to do something.
—**Eric Sevareid**

All of us in the Senate live in an iron lung—the iron lung of politics—and it is no easy task to emerge from that rarefied atmosphere in order to breathe the same fresh air our constitutents breathe.
—**John F. Kennedy**

I admit I may have dozed through some of the sessions. But I haven't had a good rest since the campaign.
—**S. I. Hayakawa**

In the Senate, you have friends; in the executive, you interface.
—**Walter Mondale**

To have true justice we must have equal harassment under the law.
—**Paul Krassner**

Influence is like a savings account. The less you use it, the more you've got.
—**Andrew Young**

There are three constant issues that have run through American politics, ever since the founding of the Republic . . . war and peace . . . bread and butter . . . and black and white.
—**Theodore White**

Sometimes it is said that a man cannot be trusted with the government of himself. Can he, then, be trusted with the government of others?
—**Walter Cronkite**

Let the people decide.
—**Stokely Carmichael**

Politics does not make strange bedfellows: it only seems that way to those who have not been following the courtship.
—**Kirkpatrick Sale**

I learned one thing in politics. If you go into it . . . then sooner or later you have to compromise. You either compromise or get out.
—**Hugh Sloan**

The first thing you do when you want to be elected is to prostitute yourself. You show me a man with courage and conviction and I'll show you a loser.
—**Ray Kroc,** chairman of McDonald's

We made no progress at all . . . and we didn't intend to. That's the function of a national committee.
—**Ronald Reagan**

The only summit meeting that can succeed is one that does not take place.
—**Barry Goldwater**

In your heart, you know I'm right.
—**Barry Goldwater,** campaign slogan, 1964

If you're not big enough to lose, you're not big enough to win.
—**Walter Reuther**

I would like to say that if we do well in 1968, we will probably not have to worry about 1984.
—**Eugene McCarthy,** in the 1968 presidential campaign

The McGovern campaign is the campaign of the three A's: acid, abortion, and amnesty.
—**Hugh Scott**

Our traditional two-party system has become a three-party system—Republican, McGovern, and Democrat.
—**Ronald Reagan**

We were always subject to this pressure from the cause people. We reacted to every threat from women, or militants, or college groups. If I had to do it all over again, I'd learn to tell them to go to hell.
—**Frank Mankiewicz,** director of George McGovern's presidential campaign, 1972

The right has a lot of discipline that the left lacks. The left always dilutes itself. Instead of merging to go after the common enemy, the left splinters, and the splinters go after one another. Meanwhile, the right keeps after its objective, pounding away, pounding away.
—**Cesar Chavez**

To treat comrades like enemies is to go over to the stand of the enemy.
—**Mao Tse-tung**

Anyone can be elected once by accident. Beginning with the second term, it's worth paying attention.
—**Sam Rayburn**

A lot of congressmen and senators like to draw their breath and their salaries and not do much else.
—**Sam Ervin**

Conferences at the top level are always courteous. Name-calling is left to the foreign ministers.
—**W. Averell Harriman**

Where else could it happen but in a country like this? To let a foreigner make peace for them, to accept a man like me—I even have a foreign accent.
—**Henry Kissinger**

Don't be humble, you're not that great.
—**Golda Meir**

We agree completely on everything, including the fact that we don't see eye to eye.
—**Henry Kissinger** and **Golda Meir**

How can anyone govern a nation that has two hundred and forty-six different kinds of cheese?
—**Charles de Gaulle**

I have not been calling the signals. I have been in the position of a lineman doing some of the downfield blocking.
—**Hubert Humphrey,** trying to dissociate himself from President Johnson's Vietnam policy during the 1968 presidential campaign

Apparently Mr. Humphrey isn't comfortable playing the Lone Ranger after playing Tonto for so long.
—**Spiro T. Agnew**

Politics, like the legal system, is dominated by old men. Old men who are also bugged by religion.
—**Mick Jagger**

I don't think politics is a workable system any more. . . . They gotta invent something better.
—**David Crosby**

Life somehow finds a way of transcending politics.
—**Norman Cousins**

We will bury you.
—**Nikita Khrushchev,** September 17, 1959

There are only two kinds of politics . . . the politics of fear and the politics of trust. One says: you are encircled by monstrous dangers. . . . The other says: the world is a baffling and hazardous place, but it can be shaped to the will of men.
—**Edmund Muskie**

Politics is sex in a hula-hoop.
—**Richard Reeves**

Politics is war without violence.
—**Stokely Carmichael**

Politicians are the same all over. They promise to build a bridge even where there is no river.
—**Nikita Khrushchev**

West Virginians have always had five friends—God Almighty, Sears Roebuck, Montgomery Ward, Carter's Little Liver Pills, and Robert C. Byrd.
—**Robert C. Byrd**

Acting is as old as mankind. . . . Politicians are actors of the first order.
—**Marlon Brando**

Being in politics is like being a football coach. You have to be smart enough to understand the game and dumb enough to think it's important.
—**Eugene McCarthy**

It is completely unimportant. That is why it is so interesting.
—**Agatha Christie**

I have often been accused of putting my foot in my mouth, but I will never put my hand in your pockets.
—**Spiro T. Agnew**

Sometimes people mistake the way I talk for what I am thinking.
—**Idi Amin**

I don't know what sort of president he'd make. He talks and talks and talks. He'd make a helluva wife.
—**Groucho Marx,** on Hubert Humphrey

I've never thought my speeches were too long: I've enjoyed them.
—**Hubert Humphrey**

In Maine we have a saying that there's no point in speaking unless you can improve on silence.
—**Edmund Muskie**

Eating words has never given me indigestion.
—**Winston Churchill**

Once you pledge, don't hedge.
—**Nikita Khrushchev**

Talking with George McGovern is like eating a Chinese meal. An hour after it's over, you wonder whether you really ate anything.
—**Eugene McCarthy**

I have no time to prepare a profound message.
—**Spiro T. Agnew**

A politician is a man who can be verbose in fewer words than anyone else.
—**Peter De Vries**

Now when I bore people at a party they think it's their fault.
—**Henry Kissinger**

A foreign secretary is forever poised between a cliché and an indiscretion.
—**Harold Macmillan**

I would not be truthful if I said I was fully qualified for the office. I do not play the piano, I seldom play golf, and I never play touch football.
—**Barry Goldwater,** on the presidency

These presidential ninnies should stick to throwing out baseballs and leave the important matters to serious people.
—**Gore Vidal**

Vote for the man who promises least; he'll be the least disappointing.
—**Bernard Baruch**

Too bad that all the people who know how to run the country are busy driving taxicabs and cutting hair.
—**George Burns**

To say you get a vote of confidence would be to say you needed a vote of confidence.
—**Andrew Young**

It is dangerous for a national candidate to say things people might remember.
—**Eugene McCarthy**

Nothing is so admirable in politics as a short memory.
—**John Kenneth Galbraith**

You must always appear right as well as be right.
—**Strom Thurmond**

If you want to talk to somebody who's not busy, call the vice president. I get plenty of time to talk to anybody about anything.
—**Walter Mondale**

The seeking of me as a candidate came like the dew in the night. It was rather gentle . . . soft, but there were signs in the morning that something had happened during the night, and so here we are.
—**Eugene McCarthy**

Seen one president, you've seen them all.
—**Henry Kissinger**

Tom Eagleton is fully qualified in mind, body, and spirit to be the vice president of the United States, and if necessary, to take over the presidency on a moment's notice.
—**George McGovern,** in the 1972 presidential campaign

I'm 1,000 percent for Tom Eagleton and I have no intention of dropping him from the ticket.
—**George McGovern**

On three occasions in my life I have voluntarily gone into hospitals as a result of nervous exhaustion and fatigue.
—**Thomas Eagleton**

My health just wasn't on my mind; it was like a broken leg that healed.
—**Thomas Eagleton,** explaining why he had not mentioned his three nervous breakdowns at the time of his nomination for vice president

It's a great country, where anybody can grow up to be president . . . except me.
—**Barry Goldwater**

Never give up and never give in.
—**Hubert Humphrey**

The party permits ordinary people to get ahead. Without the party, I couldn't be a mayor.
—**Mayor Richard Daley**

Congressmen, because they run for office every two years, are distilled politicians.
—**Richard Reeves**

There are two books that should be in the White House to read. One is the Constitution of the United States and the other is Dale Carnegie's book *How To Win Friends and Influence People.*
—**Sam Ervin**

The function of socialism is to raise suffering to a higher level.
—**Norman Mailer**

The chief problem of the lower-income farmers is poverty.
—**Nelson Rockefeller**

If you've seen one city slum, you've seen them all.
—**Spiro T. Agnew**

The streets are safe in Philadelphia, it's only the people who make them unsafe.
—**Frank Rizzo,** mayor of Philadelphia

Pessimism in our time is infinitely more respectable than optimism. . . . The man who foresees catastrophe has a gift of insight which insures that he will become a radio commentator, an editor of *Time,* or go to Congress.
—**John Kenneth Galbraith**

An optimist sees an opportunity in every calamity; a pessimist sees a calamity in every opportunity.
—**Winston Churchill**

Marvin never tells a lie if he can give you a misleading statement instead.
—**Friend** of convicted Maryland Governor Marvin Mandel

The accomplice to the crime of corruption is frequently our own indifference.
—**Bess Myerson**

Money is the mother's milk of politics.
—**Jesse Unruh**

When one hundred senators talk for thirty-seven hours, enough natural gas is produced.
—**Henry Kissinger,** on the energy filibuster

We debated this bill now for nine days. I heard the world was created in seven.
—**Robert C. Byrd**

A clean desk represents an empty mind.
—**Felix Frankfurter**

If you want to make peace, you don't talk to your friends. You talk to your enemies.
—**Moshe Dayan**

Peace is much more precious than a piece of land.
—**Anwar Sadat**

Sometimes I think this country would be better off if we could just saw off the eastern seaboard and let it float out to sea.
—**Barry Goldwater**

France cannot be France without greatness.
—**Charles de Gaulle**

To negotiate: to seek a meeting of minds without a knocking together of heads.
—**Eric Sevareid**

A Geneva settlement is like a tall mountain, full of crevices and sharp rocks. . . . You don't go to it in a straight line. You go through zigs and zags.
—**Zbigniew Brzezinski**

Nothing great will ever be achieved without great men, and men are great only if they are determined to be so.
—Charles de Gaulle

To strip our past of glory is no great loss, but to deny it honor is devastating.
—Daniel Patrick Moynihan

Nobody ever said you have to torture life to produce history.
—Jimmy Breslin

History recorded tonight would not be the same if recorded tomorrow.
—Ned Rorem

The history of things that didn't happen has never been written.
—Henry Kissinger

It's possible to dazzle a crowd if you really work at it. But that is no qualification for leadership. Hitler was a master of crowds.
—George McGovern

The real power is to make people say yes to you when they want to say no.
—Julian Bond

Propaganda is the art of persuading others of what one does not believe oneself.
Abba Eban

We should keep [the Panama Canal]. After all, we stole it fair and square.
—S. I. Hayakawa

The sword is the axis of the world, and grandeur is indivisible.
—Charles de Gaulle

Many great things indeed have been achieved by those who chose not to leap into the mainstream.
—Joan Mondale

I forsook the comfortable code of many of my predecessors, abandoned the unwritten rules—and said something.
—**Spiro T. Agnew**

It is perhaps common in the world for individuals and nations to suffer for their noble qualities more than for their ignoble ones. For nobility is an occasion for pride, the most treacherous of sentiments.
—**Daniel Patrick Moynihan**

Eggheads of the world unite; you have nothing to lose but your yolks.
—**Adlai Stevenson**

The activist cannot be a perfectionist. He's got to be a realist. And he ought to be an idealist.
—**Edmund Muskie**

If our democracy is to flourish, it must have criticism; if our government is to function, it must have dissent.
—**Henry Steele Commager**

Information is the currency of democracy.
—**Ralph Nader**

Diplomacy—the art of jumping into trouble without making a splash.
—**Art Linkletter**

Diplomacy is the art of the possible, and we have to keep readjusting our concept of what is possible.
—**Alfred L. Atherton,** assistant secretary of state for Near Eastern affairs

Diplomacy, like politics, is the art of the possible; and if we use our leverage toward an unachievable end, we will create a mess.
—**George W. Ball**

A diplomatist is a man who always remembers a woman's birthday, but never remembers her age.
—**Robert Frost**

I am as conservative as the Constitution, as liberal as Lincoln, and as progressive as Theodore Roosevelt before the Bull Moose movement.
—George Romney

If you want to get along, go along.
—Sam Rayburn

Conservatism is the worship of dead revolutions.
—Clinton Rossiter

The conservative who resists change is as valuable as the radical who proposes it.
—Will and Ariel Durant

The evolutionary process in governments continues. We have passed from Feudalism to Capitalism. Our current stage, as we all know, is Corruption.
—Jules Feiffer

I would define morality as enlightened self-interest. . . . That old Platonic ideal that there are certain pure moral forms just isn't where we are.
—Andrew Young

Your systems-analysis people have too much integrity. This is not an honorable business conducted by honorable men in an honorable way. Don't assume I'm that way and you shouldn't be.
—Henry Kissinger

The system has not failed—but some of us have failed the system.
—Edmund Muskie

Government is only as good as the men in it.
—Drew Pearson

Governments tend not to solve problems, only rearrange them.
—Ronald Reagan

I become the problem instead of the solution to the problem.
—Nelson Rockefeller

The government is becoming the family of last resort.
—Jerry Brown

I don't care what anybody says. I'm to do exactly what I want to do. If it's illegal, immoral, or fattening, Adam Powell is going to do it. I intend to live my life.
—Adam Clayton Powell

Instinct is no guide to political conduct.
—Henry Kissinger

A fellow that doesn't have any tears doesn't have any heart.
—Hubert Humphrey

66
They call me Battling Bella, Mother Courage, and a Jewish mother with more complaints than Portnoy.
—Bella Abzug

WIDE WORLD PHOTOS
99

Republicans should work for adoption of environmental programs, welfare, and revenue-sharing, and most importantly we have to keep Bella Abzug from showing up in Congress in hot-pants.
—Spiro T. Agnew

I have never met anyone who believed in democracy. I have met many who prefer it to any other form of government and who are willing to die for it. I have met many who are willing to abide by majority opinion, but I have never met anyone who believed in mass judgment. That is what democracy is.
—**Louis Nizer**

I am neither a Democrat nor a Republican. I'm a registered Whig.
—**Jack Benny**

It is a great honor to be chosen as the nation's first black congresswoman. As a United States Representative in Washington I intend to represent all the people—the blacks, the whites, the men, the women, especially the youth. There are many new ideas abroad in this country and I intend to speak for these ideas. And my voice will be heard.
—**Shirley Chisholm**

You have to adjust your running style when you're running on ice.
—**William Proxmire**

An expert gives an objective view. He gives his own view.
—**Morarji Desai,** prime minister of India

The acme of judicial distinction means the ability to look a lawyer straight in the eyes for two hours and not hear a damned word he says.
—**Chief Justice John Marshall**

When a man points a finger at someone else, he should remember that four of his fingers are pointing at himself.
—**Louis Nizer**

A jury consists of twelve persons chosen to decide who has the better lawyer.
—**Robert Frost**

A lawyer with his briefcase can steal more than a hundred men with guns.
—**Line** from *The Godfather*

The American way is first to give a man a trial and then to convict him.
—**Carl Albert**

Screw the law—you get the guy off any way you can.
—**William Kunstler**

You can't have a constitutional right to do something that is illegal.
—**Mario Cuomo**

The illegal we do immediately. The unconstitutional takes a little longer.
—**Henry Kissinger**

It is when all play safe that we create a world of utmost insecurity.
—**Dag Hammarskjöld**

What the liberal really wants is to bring about change which will not in any way endanger his position.
—**Stokely Carmichael**

A liberal is a man too broadminded to take his own side in a quarrel.
—**Robert Frost**

Hell hath no fury like a Liberal scorned!
—**Dick Gregory**

When you are right you cannot be too radical; when you are wrong, you cannot be too conservative.
—**Dr. Martin Luther King, Jr.**

The end move in politics is always to pick up a gun.
—**R. Buckminster Fuller**

Thank heaven for the military-industrial complex. Its ultimate aim is peace in our time.
—**Barry Goldwater**

We have a three-to-one advantage over the Russians, which I understand means we have the potential to kill all the Russians twice

and they have the potential to kill us about one and a quarter times.
—**Eugene McCarthy**

U.S. policy on the world scene is viewed as being neutral toward our enemy, friendly toward the neutrals, and unfriendly toward our friends.
—**Strom Thurmond**

Power . . . is the way the national ego can assert itself.
—**Norman Cousins**

I do not want to be controlled by any superpower. I myself consider myself the most powerful figure in the world.
—**Idi Amin**

In Israel, in order to be a realist, you must believe in miracles.
—**David Ben-Gurion**

The problem with me is that I am fifty or one hundred years ahead of my time. My speed is very fast. Some ministers had to drop out of my government because they could not keep up.
—**Idi Amin**

Outside the kingdom of the Lord there is no nation which is greater than any other. God and history will remember your judgment.
—**Haile Selassie**

There are no human rights in Uganda.
—**Idi Amin**

Put a bullet in a guy's head, and he won't bother you any more.
—**Attorney General William Janklow**

I captured some of the people who tried to assassinate me. I ate them before they ate me.
—**Idi Amin**

The power to blow up the world cannot be entrusted to anyone sick enough to seek it.
—**Philip Slater**

Tyrants are always assassinated too late; that is their great excuse.
—E. M. Cioran

There is no point in taking special precautions when those who want to kill me are as incompetent as those who are supposed to protect me.
—Charles de Gaulle

The most persistent threat to freedom, to the rights of Americans, is fear.
—George Meany

As long as I am mayor, there will be law and order in Chicago. Nobody is going to take over this city.
—Mayor Richard Daley

The function of liberal Republicans is to shoot the wounded after battle.
—Eugene McCarthy

You cannot shake hands with a clenched fist.
—Indira Gandhi

I am not a politician, but a professional soldier. I am, therefore, a man of few words. . . .
—Idi Amin

I do not believe in doing something just for the sake of action.
—Henry Kissinger

We have enough people who tell it like it is—now we could use a few who tell it like it can be.
—Robert Orben

We do not promise what we know cannot be delivered by man, God, or the Democratic Party.
—Lawrence O'Brien

Extremism in the defense of liberty is no vice. . . . Moderation in the pursuit of justice is no virtue.
—Barry Goldwater

The balance of power has never kept the peace in the past, and I don't see why it should in the future.
—Bertrand Russell

> 66
>
> Men struggle for worthy goals and yet they have no control over their own destinies. It all seems futile and pointless.
> —Hubert Humphrey

PHOTO COURTESY MURIEL HUMPHREY

> 99

The exercise of absolute power corrupts absolutely.
—William F. Buckley, Jr.

The hatred Americans have for their own government is pathological. . . . At one level it is simply thwarted greed: since our religion is making a buck, giving a part of that buck to any government is an act against nature.
—Gore Vidal

If you have to choose between being Don Quixote and Sancho Panza, for heaven's sake, be the Don.
—Ramsey Clark

Idealism is fine; but as it approaches reality, the cost becomes pro-
hibitive.
—**William F. Buckley, Jr.**

Life's unfairness is not irrevocable; we can help balance the scales
for others, if not always for ourselves.
—**Hubert Humphrey**

The final test of a leader is that he leaves behind in other men the
conviction and the will to carry on.
—**Walter Lippmann**

He taught us how to live and, finally, how to die.
—**Walter Mondale,** at the funeral of Hubert Humphrey

30
Sexual Politics

ELIZABETH RAY championed the cause of sexual liberation in the May 23, 1976 issue of the *Washington Post,* when she charged her boss, Wayne Hays, with conduct unbefitting a congressional representative—and a gentleman. Congressman Hays fired Miss Ray from her official position as a $14,000-a-year secretary-mistress on his staff; but the indiscretion also cost him his influential job. When asked why she had publicly disgraced her longtime lover, Miss Ray revealed the ultimate affront to a faithful mistress: he had forgotten to send her a wedding invitation—when he married another woman.

———————————

The Game women play is Men.
—**Adam Smith**

You see an awful lot of smart guys with dumb women, but you hardly ever see a smart woman with a dumb guy.
—**Erica Jong**

To a smart girl men are no problem—they're the answer.
—**Zsa Zsa Gabor**

Plain women know more about men than beautiful ones do.
—**Katharine Hepburn**

Sex appeal is 50 percent what you've got and 50 percent what people think you've got.
—**Sophia Loren**

66

If I hadn't had them, I would have had some made.
—**Dolly Parton**

DAVID GAHR, COURTESY RCA

99

A curved line is the loveliest distance between two points.
—**Mae West**

There will be sex after death—we just won't be able to feel it.
—**Lily Tomlin**

Be touchable and kissable.
—**Marabel Morgan**

The old saying, "Never mix business with pleasure," does not always apply to the business of pleasure.
—**Xaviera Hollander**

The prostitute is the only honest woman left in America.
—**Ti-Grace Atkinson**

I may never go down in history . . . but I am certainly going down on it.
—**Elizabeth Ray,** on her affair with Congressman Wayne Hays

Nothing is either all masculine or all feminine except having sex.
—**Marlo Thomas**

Even though the labels *stripper* and *congressman* are completely incongruous, there was never anything but harmony in our hearts.
—**Fanne Fox,** on her affair with Congressman Wilbur Mills

Honey, I've never taken up with a congressman in my life. I'm such a snob. I've never gone below the Senate.
—**Barbara Howar**

I don't mind living in a man's world as long as I can be a woman in it.
—**Marilyn Monroe**

Our world has changed. It's no longer a question of "Does she or doesn't she?" We all know she wants to, is about to, or does.
—**"J,"** in *The Sensuous Woman*

The whole Puritan atmosphere has one advantage. . . . It makes everything seem more exciting when you break away from it.
—**Viva**

I swallow well.
—**Linda Lovelace**

Vulgarity begins when imagination succumbs to the explicit.
—**Doris Day**

There are as many different definitions of the word obscenity as there are men.
—**Kathy Keeton**

It is better to be looked over than overlooked.
—**Mae West**

One of the paramount reasons for staying attractive is so you can have somebody to go to bed with.
—**Helen Gurley Brown**

A "prostitute" is a girl who knows how to give as well as take.
—**Xaviera Hollander**

The modern rule is that every woman must be her own chaperone.
—**Amy Vanderbilt**

For any woman to succeed in American life she must first do two things: Prepare herself for a profession, and marry a man who wants her to succeed as much as she does.
—**Cathleen Douglas,** wife of Supreme Court Justice William O. Douglas

I didn't get ahead by sleeping with people. Girls, take heart!
—**Barbara Walters**

Women who insist upon having the same options as men would do well to consider the option of being the strong, silent type.
—**Fran Lebowitz**

Men are love-starved for their fathers, are father-wounded, and no matter what women are expected to do, or what we try to do willingly, we . . . fail because it is *men* that men want to make their peace with . . . to be protected by or to be loved by.
—**Phyllis Chesler**

Men resent women because women bear kids, and seem to have this magic link with immortality that men lack. But they should stay home for a day with a kid; they'd change their minds.
—**Tuesday Weld**

To be a real woman is to bring out the best in a man.
—**Sandra Dee**

A Total Woman caters to her man's special quirks, whether it be in salads, sex, or sports.
—**Marabel Morgan**

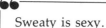

Sweaty is sexy.
—**Farrah Fawcett-Majors**

UNITED PRESS INTERNATIONAL PHOTO

With almost all doctors, population experts, and drug manufacturers male, is it really a surprise that oral contraceptives were designed for women to take and men to promote?
—**Ellen Frankfort**

Tonight, after the children are in bed, place a lighted candle on the floor and seduce him under the dining-room table.
—**Marabel Morgan**

You can call me mercenary, or call me madam, but, as I always tell my customers—just call me anytime!
—Xaviera Hollander

Striptease has always been a display of the power of suggestion.
—Fanne Fox

Variety is the spice of sex.
—Marabel Morgan

A good stripper thinks of her audience as one man whose sexual appetite she's going to whet and whose fantasies she's going to satisfy.
—Fanne Fox

I'd much rather be having fun in the bedroom instead of doing all this talking in the living room.
—Elizabeth Ray

Women are constantly being given double messages: society preaches purity and the media portrays women as nothing but sex objects.
—Ellen Frankfort

All females are born virgin and may die virgin. Virginity is eternal.
—R. Buckminster Fuller

In time we may produce a Superwoman, but in doing so we will lose the Superman, for he is only super, only at his greatest, when his spiritual capabilities are accentuated by the pure, mystical perfection of his ideal—The Virgin Woman.
—Barbara Cartland

The virgin . . . is not only an attribute of the body, it is a state of mind.
—Barbara Cartland

The only place men want depth in a woman is in her décolletage.
—Zsa Zsa Gabor

Men aren't attracted to me by my mind. They're attracted by what I don't mind.
—**Gypsy Rose Lee**

Listen, Bond, it'd take more than Crabmeat Ravigote to get me into bed.
—**Tiffany Case,** to James Bond in *Diamonds Are Forever*

Ever since Eve gave Adam the apple, there has been a misunderstanding between the sexes about gifts.
—**Nan Robertson**

All possibility of understanding is rooted in the ability to say no.
—**Susan Sontag**

The male sex, as a sex, does not universally appeal to me. I find the men today less manly; but a woman of my age is not in a position to know exactly how manly they are.
—**Katharine Hepburn**

In our family we don't divorce our men—we bury them.
—**Ruth Gordon**

Too much of a good thing can be wonderful.
—**Mae West**

31
Carter

IN JANUARY 1976, nine-year-old Amy Carter enrolled in Thaddeus Stevens Public School—becoming the first presidential child to transfer to public school in the nation's capital. Her father, Jimmy Carter, the thirty-ninth president of the United States, was elected on a platform that promised to restore the faith of the American people in the integrity of the American politician. With wife Rosalynn, Amy, his sons, daughters-in-law, and grandson in residence at the White House; Miss Lillian and brother Billy down home in Plains; and sister Ruth at her Texas retreat; Carter and his clan emerged as the most colorful and diverse First Family in our history.

> "
> I grow peanuts over in Georgia.
> —**Jimmy Carter,** in a presidential campaign speech, 1976
>
>
>
> JAY: LEVITON-ATLANTA
> "

Peanut Butter Is Love. Spread Some Around Today.
—**Sign** of the North Carolina delegation at the 1976 Democratic convention

Have faith in me. I am a Christian.
—**Jimmy Carter**

I am an engineer, I am a conservationist, and I am a scientist, an environmentalist. I am a nuclear physicist, I am an outdoorsman, I am a Christian, and I don't see any conflict among these things.
—**Jimmy Carter**

I have never claimed to be better or wiser than any other person. I think my greatest strength is that I am an ordinary man.
—**Jimmy Carter**

I'm not saying I'm the best qualified person in this room to be president. Many of you out there might be able to do just as good a job as I can, or better . . . but I sure do thank y'all for not running this year. There are enough candidates already.
—Jimmy Carter

We should live our lives as though Christ were coming this afternoon.
—Jimmy Carter

Christ says, don't consider yourself better than someone else because one guy screws a whole bunch of women, while the other guy is loyal to his wife.
—Jimmy Carter

I've looked on a lot of women with lust. I've committed adultery in my heart many times. This is something God recognizes I will do—and I have done it—and God forgives me for it. But that doesn't mean that I condemn someone who not only looks on a woman with lust but who leaves his wife and shacks up with someone out of wedlock.
—Jimmy Carter

He says his lust is in his heart. I hope it's a little lower.
—Shirley MacLaine, on Jimmy Carter

The first thing Jimmy's gonna do when he gets inaugurated is pardon me.
—Billy Carter

How could Jimmy ever criticize me? I'm his mama.
—Lillian Carter

I got a mama who joined the Peace Corps when she was sixty-eight. I got one sister who's a Holy Roller preacher. Another wears a helmet and rides a motorcycle. And my brother thinks he's going to be president. So that makes me the only sane one in the family.
—Billy Carter

Sure, I'm for helping the elderly. I'm going to be old myself someday.
—Lillian Carter

Jimmy used to drink liquor. Now he's running for president and he drinks Scotch, and I've never trusted a Scotch-drinker.
—**Billy Carter**

I think he rented the family. I don't believe Lillian is his mother. I don't believe Billy is his brother. They're all from Central Casting.
—**Johnny Carson**

People are the same most everywhere you go. . . . They just make their living in different ways.
—**Rosalynn Carter**

Don't mess with me. I know people in high places. I know Amy.
—**Midge Costanza**

This administration doesn't have an enemies list; it has a friends list.
—**James Abourezk,** former state senator of South Dakota

The first one to go down was Ed Muskie. He sidled up to Rosalynn Carter and said, "I just love green-eyed peas." John Glenn told Jimmy Carter, "You know, I've never seen a peanut tree in my life." Frank Church said, "I've never been in Georgia, but I had a relative in the army down there once—General Sherman." When I arrived in Plains, Jimmy Carter told me, "You just keep your mouth shut, and the job is yours."
—**Walter Mondale**

When I am your president, I hope you'll come see me. Please don't leave me up there in the White House all by myself.
—**Jimmy Carter**

I worship the very quicksand he walks on.
—**Art Buchwald,** on Jimmy Carter

If I ever tell a lie, if I ever mislead you, if I ever betray a trust or a confidence, I want you to come and take me out of the White House.
—**Jimmy Carter**

Jimmy says he'll never tell a lie. Well, I lie all the time. I have to—to balance the family ticket.
—**Lillian Carter**

I have nothing against a community that's made up of people who are Polish or Czechoslovakian or French-Canadian, or blacks who are trying to maintain the ethnic purity of their neighborhoods.
—**Jimmy Carter,** in a campaign interview with the *New York Daily News*

I'm just a country boy and you city boys never did understand the way we talk.
—**Jimmy Carter**

Yes, sir! I'm a real Southern boy. I got a red neck, white socks, and Blue Ribbon beer.
—**Billy Carter**

Love must be aggressively translated into simple justice.
—**Jimmy Carter**

The Southern liberal has a certain kind of integrity that's almost impossible to achieve in the North.
—**Tom Hayden**

The tax system is a disgrace to the human race. I believe all income should be treated the same. It's a scandal that a businessman can deduct his fifty-dollar lunch but a worker can't deduct the sandwich in his lunch pail.
—**Jimmy Carter**

I don't care how many martinis anyone has with lunch. But I do care who picks up the check.
—**Jimmy Carter**

The sad duty of politics is to establish justice in a sinful world.
—**Jimmy Carter,** quoting Reinhold Niebuhr, during the 1976 presidential election campaign

I have a vision of an America that is, in Bob Dylan's phrase, busy being born, not dying.
—**Jimmy Carter**

32

66 ———————————————————————————————— 99

Literary Set

EDITOR MAXWELL PERKINS might not recognize his "genteel profession" today. Publishing has grown from a cottage industry to a sophisticated multimillion-dollar business dominated by huge conglomerates—complete with instant paperbacks, media tie-ins, and staggering paperback sales. In the 1970s, three novels received the highest sums ever paid by paperback publishers: *Ragtime*, by E. L Doctorow—$1.85 million; *The Thorn Birds*, by Colleen Mc-Cullough—$1.9 million; and *Fools Die*, by Mario Puzo—$2.55 million.

———————————————

Hell hath no fury like a hustler with a literary agent.
—**Frank Sinatra**

The relationship of an agent to a publisher is that of a knife to a throat.
—**Marvin Josephson,** superagent

Anybody can make an easy deal, but only a true agent can sell a dog.
—**Irving (Swifty) Lazar**

I love this business. There are two big kicks. One is selling something for a person who's never sold before. And the other is selling something nobody wants.
—**Scott Meredith,** literary agent

Our goal is to conglomeratize the world.
—**Sam Weisbord,** president, William Morris Agency

Trust your publisher and he can't fail to treat you generously.
—**Alfred A. Knopf**

We have people earning $250,000 a book thinking they're failures.
—**Joni Evans,** associate publisher, Simon & Schuster

The dubious privilege of a freelance writer is he's given the freedom to starve anywhere.
—**S. J. Perelman**

Write out of love; write out of instinct; write out of reason. But always for money.
—**Louis Untermeyer**

I always start a book for money. If you're married five times you have to.
—**Norman Mailer**

Art is as unimportant as banking, unless it comes from a spirit in free play—then it really is banking.
—**Lawrence Durrell**

How much do you think I'll get for my autobiography?
—**Arthur Bremmer,** after attempting to assassinate George Wallace in Laurel, Maryland, May 1972

I wonder whether what we are publishing now is worth cutting down trees to make paper for the stuff.
—**Richard Brautigan**

They'd publish my parking tickets.
—**Sylvester Stallone,** on books by superstars

A writer is someone who always sells. An author is one who writes a book that makes a big splash.
—**Mickey Spillane**

The rules seem to be these: if you have written a successful novel, everyone invites you to write short stories. If you have written some good short stories, everyone wants you to write a novel. But nobody wants anything until you have already proved yourself by being published somewhere else.
—**James Michener**

Nothing stinks like a pile of unpublished writing.
—**Sylvia Plath**

Not yet published a writer lies in the womb . . . waiting for the privilege to breathe. Outside is the great, exhaling company of those who have expressed.
—**Hortense Calisher**

The idea is to get the pencil moving quickly.
—**Bernard Malamud**

A still umbilicaled book is no more formed than a fetus.
—**William Gass**

A painful birth, a difficult baby, but a kind daughter.
—**Vladimir Nabokov,** on *Lolita*

The first novel is a good place to put things that would be awkward to use elsewhere.
—**Peter Prescott**

First publication is a pure, carnal leap into that dark which one dreams is life.
—**Hortense Calisher**

Out of the old gut onto the goddamn page.
—**Terry Southern**

I love being a writer. What I can't stand is the paperwork.
—**Peter De Vries**

Having been unpopular in high school is not just cause for book publication.
—**Fran Lebowitz**

If you can't be funny, be interesting.
—**Harold Ross,** founder of the *New Yorker*

A bad book is as much a labor to write as a good one, it comes as sincerely from the author's soul.
—**Aldous Huxley**

Good writing is true writing. If a man is making a story up it will be true in proportion to the amount of knowledge of life that he has had and how conscientious he is; so that when he makes something up it is as it would truly be.
—**Ernest Hemingway**

No complete son of a bitch ever wrote a good sentence.
—**Malcolm Cowley**

All good art is an indiscretion.
—**Tennessee Williams**

If truth is fact, then all art . . . lies, but by extension sparks true.
—**Ned Rorem**

Man's task is to make of himself a work of art.
—**Henry Miller**

Life is the only sentence which doesn't end with a period.
—**Lois Gould**

Wrestling with illusion is part of writing. Invent illusion, and you murder it.
—**Bernard Malamud**

It is now life and not art that requires the willing suspension of disbelief.
—**Lionel Trilling**

Writing is a suspension of life in order to re-create life.
—**John McPhee**

The novel is rescued life.
—**Hortense Calisher**

The novel is something that never was before and will not be again.
—**Eudora Welty**

The complete novelist would come into the world with a catalog of qualities something like this. He would own the concentration of a Trappist monk, the organizational ability of a Prussian field marshal, the insight into human relations of a Viennese psychiatrist, the discipline of a man who prints the Lord's Prayer on the head of a pin, the exquisite sense of timing of an Olympic gymnast, and by the way, a natural instinct and flair for exceptional use of language.
—**Leon Uris**

A writer is not someone who expresses his thoughts, his passion, or his imagination in sentences but someone who thinks sentences. A Sentence-Thinker.
—**Roland Barthes**

Before I start to write, I always treat myself to a nice dry martini. Just one, to give me the courage to get started. After that, I am on my own.
—**E.B. White**

I do not write for a select minority . . . nor for that adulated platonic entity known as "The Masses." Both abstractions, so dear to the demagogue, I disbelieve in. I write for myself and my friends and I write to ease the passing of time.
—**Jorge Luis Borges**

Art makes no laws—only very difficult complicated suggestions.
—**John Gardner**

It is the function of art to renew our perception. What we are familiar with we cease to see. The writer shakes up the familiar scene, and as if by magic, we see a new meaning in it.
—**Anaïs Nin**

The immature artist imitates. Mature artists steal.
—**Lionel Trilling**

I do borrow from other writers, *shamelessly!* I can only say in my defense, like the woman brought before the judge on a charge of kleptomania, "I do steal; but, Your Honor, only from the very best stores."
—**Thornton Wilder**

A successful book cannot afford to be more than 10 percent new.
—**Marshall McLuhan**

The wastepaper basket is a writer's best friend.
—**Isaac Bashevis Singer**

Art is too long and life is too short.
—**Grace Paley**

[Art is] the reasoned derangement of the senses.
—**Kenneth Rexroth**

The only people for me are the mad ones, the ones who are mad to live, mad to talk, mad to be saved . . . the ones who . . . burn, burn, burn, burn.
—**Jack Kerouac**

That's not writing, that's typing!
—**Truman Capote,** on Jack Kerouac

I have never seen a more lucid, better balanced, mad mind than mine.
—**Vladimir Nabokov**

The mind is a prolix gut.
—**Stanley Kunitz**

I am the beneficiary of a lucky break in the genetic sweepstakes.
—**Isaac Asimov**

Writing is a yoga that invokes Lord mind.
—**Allen Ginsberg**

Unlike God, the novelist does not start with nothing and make something of it. He starts with himself as nothing and makes something of the nothing with the things at hand.
—**Walker Percy**

A novelist is a person who lives in other people's skins.
—**E. L. Doctorow**

I am an invisible man. No, I am not a spook . . . nor am I one of your Hollywood-movie ectoplasms. I am a man of substance, of flesh and bone, fiber and liquids—and I might even be said to possess a mind. I am invisible, understand, simply because people refuse to see me.
—**Ralph Ellison,** in *Invisible Man*

Fiction is our only continuous history of our struggle to be illustrious.
—**John Cheever**

A style is a writer's passport to posterity.
—**Leon Edel**

Creativity is a yearning for immortality.
—**Rollo May**

There is no way of being a creative writer in America without being a loser.
—**Nelson Algren**

You don't die in the United States, you underachieve.
—**Jerzy Kosinski**

I am marked like a road map from head to toe with my repressions. You can travel the length and breadth of my body over superhighways of shame and inhibition and fear.
—**Alexander Portnoy,** in *Portnoy's Complaint*

One reason the human race has such a low opinion of itself is that it gets so much of its wisdom from writers.
—**Wilfrid Sheed**

If success is corrupting, failure is narrowing.
—**Stephen Spender**

The child in me is delighted. The adult in me is skeptical.
—**Saul Bellow,** upon receiving the 1976 Nobel Prize for literature

Success has been a lobotomy to my past.
—**Norman Mailer**

If you wander around in enough confusion, you will soon find enlightenment.
—**Digby Diehl**

Life is an unanswered question, but let's believe in the dignity and importance of the question.
—**Tennessee Williams**

For most people, fiction is history; fiction is history without tables, graphs, dates, imports, edicts, evidence, laws; history without hiatus—intelligible, simple, smooth.
—**William Gass**

It is the way of the world that goodness is often repaid with badness. This is what I have told you as a story.
—**Alex Haley,** in *Roots*

Stories ought to judge and interpret the world.
—**Cynthia Ozick**

If you're looking for messages, try Western Union.
—**Ernest Hemingway**

Dogmas always die of dogmatism.
—**Anaïs Nin**

Occasionally we should allow the trite to tease us into thought, for such old friends, the clichés in our life, are the only strangers we can know.
—**William Gass**

I've made characters live, so that people talk about them at cocktail parties, and that, to me, is what counts.
—**Jacqueline Susann**

All literature is gossip.
—**Truman Capote**

Capote should be heard, not read.
—**Gore Vidal,** on Truman Capote

This may be the last generation of writers; in the future, everything may be taped.
—**Clive Barnes**

Literature these days is so sex-happy that I can't always keep my perversions straight.
—**Clifton Fadiman**

If your sexual fantasies were truly of interest to others, they would no longer be fantasies.
—**Fran Lebowitz**

A historical romance is the only kind of book where chastity really counts.
—**Barbara Cartland**

Of all forms of genius, goodness has the longest awkward age.
—**Thornton Wilder**

Talent is what you possess; genius is what possesses you.
—**Malcolm Cowley**

You can lie to your wife or your boss, but you cannot lie to your typewriter. Sooner or later you must reveal your true self in your pages.
—**Leon Uris**

The writer . . . is a person who talks to himself, or better, who talks in himself.
—**Malcolm Cowley**

An essayist is a lucky person who has found a way to discourse without being interrupted.
—**Charles Poore**

I am, at heart, a tiresome nag complacently positive that there is no human problem which could not be solved if people would simply do as I advise.
—**Gore Vidal**

Living in your own literary confines is like falling in love with your own relatives.
—**Andrei Voznesenski**

If you have one strong idea, you can't help repeating it and embroidering it. Sometimes I think that authors should write one novel and then be put in a gas chamber.
—**John P. Marquand**

Good writers are monotonous, like good composers. Their truth is self-repeating. . . . They keep trying to perfect their understanding of the one problem they were born to understand.
—**Alberto Moravia**

The true function of a writer is to produce a masterpiece and . . . no other task is of any consequence.
—**Cyril Connolly**

Clear prose indicates the absence of thought.
—**Marshall McLuhan**

Be obscure clearly.
—**E. B. White**

You never have to change anything you got up in the middle of the night to write.
—**Saul Bellow**

Listen carefully to first criticisms made of your work. Note just what it is about your work that the critics don't like—then cultivate it. That's the only part of your work that's individual and worth keeping.
—**Jean Cocteau**

Asking a working writer what he thinks about critics is like asking a lamppost what it feels about dogs.
—**John Osborne**

Reading reviews of your own book is . . . a no-win game. If the review is flattering, one tends to feel vain and uneasy. If it is bad, one tends to feel exposed, found out. Neither feeling does you any good.
—**Walker Percy**

Reviewers are not born but made, and they are made by editors.
—**Anthony Burgess**

There is no such thing as a New York intellectual establishment. It just looks that way from the outside.
—**Jason Epstein,** editor-in-chief, Random House

Every time I open a book, I risk my life. . . . Every work of imagination offers another view of life, an invitation to spend a few days inside someone else's emotions.
—**Anatole Broyard**

A critic is a man who knows the way but can't drive the car.
—**Kenneth Tynan**

The critic's job is . . . confining, frequently enervating, often beguiling, and generally exposed. There is some resemblance to working in a coal mine. The work is done in the dark, it is done alone, and the roof keeps falling in.
—**Richard Eder**

There is in every reviewer an occasional temptation to assume the role of a bottle of Johnson's No-Roach with the spray applicator.
—**John Leonard**

You don't so much review a play as draw up a crushing brief against it.
—**Edmund Wilson**

Critics of literature have the same essential function as teachers of literature: this is not to direct the judgment of the audience, but to assist the audience in those disciplines of reading on which any meaningful judgment must rest.
—**Mark Schorer**

Writing is: the science of the various blisses of language.
—**Roland Barthes**

The poet marries the language, and out of this marriage the poem is born.
—**W. H. Auden**

> When power corrupts, poetry cleanses.
> —**John F. Kennedy**

UNITED PRESS INTERNATIONAL PHOTO

There's no money in poetry, but then there's no poetry in money either.
—**Robert Graves**

The blood jet is poetry/There is no stopping it.
—**Sylvia Plath**

Perfect things in poetry do not seem strange, they seem inevitable.
—**Jorge Luis Borges**

Poetry is mostly hunches.
—**John Ashbery**

Writing free verse is like playing tennis with the net down.
—**Robert Frost**

Two poetries are now competing, a cooked and a raw. The cooked, marvelously expert, often seems laboriously concocted to be tasted and digested by a graduate seminar. The raw, huge, blood-drip-

ping gobbet of unseasoned experience are dished up for midnight listeners.
—**Robert Lowell,** on accepting the National Book Award, 1960

Lying of an inspired, habitual, inventive kind, given a personality, a form, and a rhythm, is mainly what poetry is.
—**James Dickey**

Poetry is language surprised in the act of changing into meaning.
—**Stanley Kunitz**

I see no reason for calling my work poetry except that there is no other category in which to put it.
—**Marianne Moore,** on accepting the National Book Award

I intend to become America's black female Proust.
—**Maya Angelou**

A poet's autobiography is his poetry. Anything else can only be a footnote.
—**Yevgeny Yevtushenko**

To become a poet is to take the whole field of human knowledge and human desire for one's province. . . . Yes, but this field can only be covered by continual inner abdications.
—**Lawrence Durrell**

In every generation there has to be some fool who will speak the truth as he sees it.
—**Boris Pasternak**

In Russia when you answer questions, you may come to an unfortunate conclusion.
—**Aleksandr Solzhenitzyn**

Death is a metaphor; nobody dies to himself.
—**Lawrence Durrell**

I believe that man will not merely endure; he will prevail.
—**William Faulkner,** on accepting the Nobel Prize for literature

A writer who does not passionately believe in the perfectibility of man has no dedication nor any membership in literature.
—**John Steinbeck**

An era can be said to end when its basic illusions are exhausted.
—**Arthur Miller**

There was only one catch and that was Catch-22, which specified that a concern for one's own safety in the face of dangers that were real and immediate was the process of a rational mind.
—**Joseph Heller,** in *Catch-22*

Satire is moral rage transformed into comic art.
—**Philip Roth**

The real comic novel has to do with man's recognition of his unimportance in the universe.
—**Anthony Burgess**

The trouble with our age is all signpost and no destination.
—**Louis Kronenberger**

A biographer is like a contractor who builds roads: It's terribly messy, mud everywhere, and when you get done, people travel over the road at a fast clip.
—**Arthur Wilson**

The mind of the poacher runneth not to the even split.
—**Carroll O'Connor,** on Arthur Marx's announcement that he
    would write an unauthorized biography of O'Connor

I've always believed in writing without a collaborator, because where two people are writing the same book, each believes he gets all the worries and only half the royalties.
—**Agatha Christie**

All art is autobiographical; the pearl is the oyster's autobiography.
—**Federico Fellini**

Only when one has lost all curiosity about the future has one reached the stage to write an autobiography.
—**Evelyn Waugh**

The language is no longer lived; it is merely spoken.
—George Steiner

Slang is the language that takes off its coat, spits on its hands, and goes to work.
—Carl Sandburg

Being a writer in the South has its special miseries, which include isolation, madness, tics, amnesia, alcoholism, lust, and loss of ordinary powers of speech. One may go for days without saying a word.
—Walker Percy

When I'm asked why Southern writers particularly have a penchant for writing about freaks, I say it's because we are still able to recognize one.
—Flannery O'Connor

Why has the South produced so many good writers? Because we got beat.
—Walker Percy

A Yankee, a real Yankee—that's a person who's an idealist even after he's come to see how hopeless life is.
—John Hersey

Look, Chief, you can't go off half-cocked looking for vengeance against a fish. That shark isn't evil, it's not a murderer. It's just obeying its own instincts. Trying to get retribution against a fish is crazy.
—Matt Hooper, to Martin Brody in *Jaws*

The American novel is a conquest of the frontier; as it describes experience it creates it.
—Ralph Ellison

When you reread a classic you do not see more in the book than you did before; you see more in you than there was before.
—Clifton Fadiman

It is not true that we have only one life to live; if we can read, we can live as many more lives and as many kinds as we wish.
—S. I. Hayakawa

33
"A Touch of Class"

THE FEBRUARY 23, 1969 GIG at the Fillmore East was an historic encounter. Classical pianist Lorin Hollander, then twenty-four, in sideburns and Greenwich Village chic, played Bach's Partita no. 6 and Debussy's "Fireworks," winning a standing ovation from hundreds of hippies.

The artistic triumph marked the symbolic resolution of a long-standing schism between high- and lowbrows. By 1970, popular culture had integrated classical and commercial sensibilities into a uniquely American art. The signs of this cultural integration were visible in the "crossovers" of the 1960s. Leonard Bernstein came down from the podium of the New York Philharmonic to herald the Beatles as classic masters of modern music; Beverly Sills, America's home-grown prima donna, proclaimed herself "the Beatles of the opera"; and Andy Warhol, the leading underground artist, showed the beautiful people that a can of Campbell's soup can be chic.

In the future everyone will be famous for fifteen minutes.
—**Andy Warhol**

Celebrity is like having an extra lump of sugar in your coffee.
—**Mikhail Baryshnikov**

We are all more or less schlemiels.
—**Jacques Lipchitz**

Charm is a way of getting the answer yes without having asked any clear question.
—**Albert Camus**

If you can sell green toothpaste in this country, you can sell opera.
—**Sarah Caldwell**

Pop music is the hamburger of every day.
—**Pierre Boulez**

The Philharmonic is like marriage. I have to sneak little flings on the side.
—**Leonard Bernstein**

I'm the Beatles of the opera.
—**Beverly Sills**

[Pop art is] the use of commercial art as subject matter in painting.
—**Roy Lichtenstein**

The purpose of art is always, ultimately, to give pleasure—though our sensibilities may take time to catch up with the forms of pleasure that art in a given time may offer.
—**Susan Sontag**

The meaning of my work is that it is industrial; it's what all the world will soon become.
—**Roy Lichtenstein**

Pop art is the inedible raised to the unspeakable.
—**Leonard Baskin**

Having the critics praise you is like having the hangman say you've got a pretty neck.
—**Eli Wallach**

An artist is born kneeling; he fights to stand. A critic, by nature of the judgment seat, is born sitting.
—**Hortense Calisher**

The worst thing that can happen to an actor is to be hailed as a genius the first time he walks onstage.
—**John Wood**

If society were different, we might be content just to do something well. But no one is pleased to simply do what they do. What's important for us is always what doesn't exist.
—**Jasper Johns**

My total conscious search in life has been for a new seeing, a new image, a new insight. This search not only includes the object, but the in-between place.
—**Louise Nevelson**

Architecture should be dedicated to keeping the outside out and the inside in.
—**Leonard Baskin**

Good architecture lets nature in.
—**I. M. Pei**

A doctor can bury his mistakes but an architect can only advise his client to plant vines.
—**Frank Lloyd Wright**

Painting is an indoor art. You don't put a Rembrandt on the lawn.
—**Henry Moore**

I am not interested in relationships of color or anything else. . . . I am interested only in expressing the basic human emotions—tragedy, ecstasy, doom.
—**Mark Rothko**

Strong and convincing art has never arisen from theories.
—**Mary Wigman**

I should have the courage of my lack of convictions.
—**Tom Stoppard**

A picture lives by companionship. It dies by the same token. It is therefore risky to send it out into the world. How often it must be permanently impaired by the eyes of the unfeeling.
—**Mark Rothko**

We all know that art is not truth. Art is a lie that makes us realize truth.
—**Pablo Picasso**

Abstract art is uniquely modern. . . . It is a fundamentally romantic response to modern life—rebellious, individualistic, unconventional, sensitive, irritable.
—**Robert Motherwell**

Abstract Art: A product of the untalented, sold by the unprincipled to the utterly bewildered.
—**Al Capp**

I am opposed to painting concerned with conceptions of simplification. Everything looks very busy to me.
—**Jasper Johns**

I like painting on a square because you don't have to decide whether it should be longer-longer or shorter-shorter or longer-shorter; it's just a square.
—**Andy Warhol**

Nothing is inherently valueless. It depends on how far it goes and what the intent is.
—**Jill Clayburgh**

You can't live unless you know what you'll stop at.
—**Mike Nichols**

Take an object. Do something to it. Do something else to it.
—**Credo of Jasper Johns**

In art spontaneity must always be calculated.
—**Ned Rorem**

Painting is self-discovery.
—Jackson Pollock

The value of doing self-portraits for me has always been the reaffirmation that I do exist.
—Jim Dine

When I was a child my mother said to me, "If you become a soldier you'll be a general. If you become a monk you'll end up as the pope." Instead I became a painter and wound up as Picasso.
—Pablo Picasso

If you set out deliberately to make a masterpiece, how will you ever get it finished?
—George Balanchine

The crane is my paintbrush.
—Mark di Suvero

True strength is delicate.
—Louise Nevelson

The more minimal the art, the more maximum the explanation.
—Hilton Kramer

Everybody wants to understand painting. Why is there no attempt to understand the song of the birds? Why does one love a night, a flower, everything that surrounds a man, without trying to understand it all?
—Pablo Picasso

The highest purpose is to have no purpose at all.
—John Cage

Flesh was the reason why oil painting was invented.
—Willem de Kooning

Sexual obsessions are the basis of artistic creation.
—Salvador Dali

Pop is either hard-core or hard-edge.
—**Robert Indiana**

It would be terrific if everybody was alike. The reason I'm painting this way is because I want to be a machine.
—**Andy Warhol**

Everyone has his reasons.
—**Jean Renoir**

Only the upright heart that has its own logic and its own reason is free.
—**Marc Chagall**

No one should be called a defector. I'd like to be called a cultural exchange.
—**Mikhail Baryshnikov**

Communism stifles art. There is little important art you can cite from Communist countries. Solzhenitzyn is not nearly as impressive as Tolstoi.
—**Richard Nixon**

No matter what side of an argument you're on, you always find some people on your side that you wish were on the other side.
—**Jascha Heifetz**

My muse must come to me on "union" time.
—**George Balanchine**

Great artists are people who find the way to be themselves in their art.
—**Margot Fonteyn**

I do not try to dance better than anyone else. I only try to dance better than myself.
—**Mikhail Baryshnikov**

My feet are dogs.
—**Rudolf Nureyev**

If you want a place in the sun, you've got to put up with a few blisters.
—**Abigail Van Buren**

It is very peaceful to be able to live for your work alone. The self-denial, the sacrifices that our work demands are all compensated for by that lovely serenity of giving yourself up to dance.
—**Edward Villella**

Every dancer lives on the threshold of chucking it.
—**Judith Jamison**

66

Ballet is woman.
—**George Balanchine**

MARTHA SWOPE

99

The cello is like a beautiful woman who has not grown older, but younger with time, more slender, more supple, more graceful.
—**Pablo Casals**

God creates, woman inspires, and man assembles.
—**George Balanchine**

The artist doesn't see things as they are, he sees things as he is.
—**Robert Beverly Hale**

Nothing is more revealing than movement.
—**Martha Graham**

Half the world wants to be like Thoreau at Walden worrying about the noise of traffic on the way to Boston; the other half use up their lives being part of that noise. I like the second half.
—**Franz Kline**

Our age is precisely the age of the industrialization of fantasy.
—**André Malraux**

Needing to have reality confirmed and experience enhanced by photographs is an esthetic consumerism to which everyone is now addicted. Industrial societies turn their citizens into image-junkies; it is the most irresistible form of mental pollution.
—**Susan Sontag**

One has a nose. The nose scents and it chooses. An artist is simply a kind of pig snouting truffles.
—**Igor Stravinsky**

The contemporary hunger for the irrational is always keenest before a cultural dining table offering only the cold and unsubstantial left-overs of art and literature.
—**Salvador Dali**

All it takes to be a restaurant critic in Portland is being able to tell which frozen cheesecake is Sara Lee.
—**Gloria Russakov**

A tablecloth restaurant is still one of the great rewards of civilization.
—**Harry Golden**

It's a naïve domestic Burgundy without any breeding, but I think
you'll be amused by its presumption.
—**James Thurber**

Any sort of pretension induces mediocrity in art and life alike.
—**Margot Fonteyn**

Surrealists . . . are not quite artists, nor are we really scientists; we
are caviar . . . the extravagance and intelligence of taste.
—**Salvador Dali**

Music that is born complex is not inherently better or worse than
music that is born simple.
—**Aaron Copland**

66

After silence that which comes nearest to expressing the inex·
pressible is music.
—**Aldous Huxley**

PHOTO COURTESY RCA

99

Since we cannot hope for order, let us withdraw with style from the chaos.
—Tom Stoppard

If this word "music" is sacred and reserved for eighteenth- and nineteenth-century instruments, we can substitute a more meaningful term: organization of sound.
—John Cage

Cacophony is hard to swallow.
—Duke Ellington

When in doubt, sing loud.
—Robert Merrill

Composing is like making love to the future.
—Lukas Foss

Music is a language without a dictionary whose symbols are interpreted by the listener according to some unwritten Esperanto of the emotions.
—Aaron Copland

Composers shouldn't think too much—it interferes with their plagiarism.
—Howard Dietz

A good composer does not imitate, he steals.
—Igor Stravinsky

Now we sit through Shakespeare in order to recognize the quotations.
—Orson Welles

A fine artist is one who makes familiar things new and new things familiar.
—Louis Nizer

People who see a drawing in the *New Yorker* will think automatically that it's funny because it is a cartoon. If they see it in a mu-

seum, they think it is artistic; and if they find it in a fortune cookie, they think it is a prediction.
—**Saul Steinberg**

The highest vocation of photography is to explain man to man.
—**Susan Sontag**

A photograph is a secret about a secret. The more it tells you the less you know.
—**Diane Arbus**

Being photographed is a performance.
—**Henry Geldzahler,** former curator of twentieth-century art at the Metropolitan Museum of Art

The camera makes everyone a tourist in other people's reality, and eventually in one's own.
—**Susan Sontag**

The middle class are as noble a subject as the Medicis or the farm workers. They're so uncertain about their own identities that they change lifestyles every twelve months. I have compassion for them because I'm one of them.
—**Paul Mazursky**

It gave me great pleasure to think that I could take wood, make it good, and make people like Rockefeller buy it with paper money.
—**Louise Nevelson**

Great artists need great clients.
—**I. M. Pei**

The opera is like a husband with a foreign title: expensive to support, hard to understand, and therefore a supreme social challenge.
—**Cleveland Amory**

Opera has no business making money.
—**Sir Rudolf Bing**

The Metropolitan Opera is not a place of entertainment but a place of penance.
—**Sir Thomas Beecham**

Music is the sole domain in which man realizes the present.
—Igor Stravinsky

Playing "bop" is like playing Scrabble with all the vowels missing.
—Duke Ellington

Pop drives jazz back underground.
—Pauline Kael

The only true comment on a piece of music is another piece of music.
—Igor Stravinsky

Music is a means of Rapid Transportation.
—John Cage

When one burns one's bridges, what a very nice fire it makes.
—Dylan Thomas

To be deprived of art and left alone with philosophy is to be close to Hell.
—Igor Stravinsky

What do you do with your beautiful, young, freckled mind?
—Duke Ellington

Index

ABOUT THE AUTHOR

BARBARA ROWES has been a dance critic for the *Los Angeles Times*, the *Toronto Globe and Mail*, and the *Baltimore Sun*, and a cultural critic and reporter for the *Washington Post* and the *New York Times*. Her articles, on everything from psychology to contemporary literature to rock music, have appeared in a variety of national magazines, including *People, New Times, Glamour, Viva*, and *Apartment Life*.

Barbara Rowes received her B.A. in English and classics from New York University, her M.A. in writing from Johns Hopkins, and her Ph.D. in Renaissance literature from the State University of New York at Buffalo. In addition, she has been an assistant professor of both modern dance and journalism at California State University. Her hobbies include reading quotation books and discovering elegant places to eat breakfast. She has accomplished all this in the space of three decades, and is herself an anthology of contemporary sensibility.